POGO
EVEN BETTER

Edited by

Mrs. Walt Kelly *and* Bill Crouch, Jr.

A FIRESIDE BOOK
PUBLISHED BY SIMON & SCHUSTER, INC.
NEW YORK

To "Flicky" Ford and John Horn,
long-standing Kelly friends through thick and thin

A Fireside Book
Published by Simon & Schuster, Inc.
Simon & Schuster Building
Rockefeller Center
1230 Avenue of the Americas
New York, New York 10020
FIRESIDE and colophon are registered trademarks of Simon & Schuster, Inc.
Manufactured in the United States of America
Printed and bound by The Murray Printing Company, Inc.

3 4 5 6 7 8 9 10

ISBN: 0-671-50473-8

CONTENTS

INTRODUCTION

Way back before I was a cartoonist – when I was nothing more than a cartoon – I was introduced to the works of Walt Kelly by my mother, who would read *Pogo* to my brother and me at bedtimes.

Long before I could grasp the satirical significance of his stuff I was enchanted by Kelly's magnificent artwork. His mastery of brush and ink led me down the spattered trail to the smudgy craft.

He tricked me, though.

Now I'm stuck with hundreds of cantankerous brushes that refuse to work as well as his always did, and I'm locked into a never-ending quest for just the right combination of pen, brush, paper, and ink that will make it all look as free and easy as Walt made it look. His mastery of black and white was so complete that I remember being disappointed with the Sunday *Pogo* pages – the color always seemed to get in the way of the drawing.

We'll never see anything like *Pogo* again in the funnies, I'm afraid. Not only are we unlikely to run across a comic genius like Walt Kelly's again, but the advances in high tech printing and aggressive accounting procedures have made it possible for today's newspapers to cram four or five comics onto a single Sunday comic page. If Walt were alive today he'd be kicking. Not only would his great detail work be reduced to a smear the size of an airmail stamp, but he'd be getting calls from his editors to "make the words bigger."

What words they were. The conversations among the creatures of the Okefenokee were wonderfully gentle mockeries of the inept attempts of us humans to communicate with each other. And the comedy was sharper than most things ever done on the tube or screen or stage. The bat brothers routines rival the vaudeville classics.

Luckily, thanks to collections such as this one, and the dedication of Pogophiles such as Bill Crouch, we can keep Walt's work with us to enjoy and to pass on.

And, if I ever get to the point where I think I've figured out how this damn brush works, I can open this book and find out I'm not even close.

Thanks, Walt.

Jeff MacNelly

Possum Power!

Given the popularity of cat comic strips, it seemed a good idea to hype the concept that if cats have nine lives, then possums have ten. While this was originally meant as a joke, it has become the truth. Pogo Possum is virtually indestructible thanks to his loyal fans.

I have also been gratified to discover that Pogophile tendencies must in part be passed on genetically. There are many Pogophiles whose parents taught them "Deck Us All With Boston Charlie" and whose grandchildren are learning the song today.

If any one word can sum up this remarkable comic strip about the denizens of the Okefenokee Swamp it is quality. Walt Kelly wrote and drew a comic strip of such quality it has become a timeless classic.

Pogo Even Better is a compilation of Pogo dailies from 1949 and 1950, previously not reprinted Sunday pages, photos of Walt Kelly, and even a "new" half verse of Boston Charlie. It is the companion volume to *The Best of Pogo: Collected from The Okefenokee Star* (1982).

What is Possum Power? It is simply the love and support of Walt Kelly's many fans for a little ol' possum named Pogo, Albert the Alligator, Howland Owl, Porky Pine, Churchy La Femme, and a cast of uncounted swamp critters.

With reprints of Kelly's early work (Life of P.T. Barnum, fantasy drawings, Mother Goose illustrations) I have tried to illustrate the progression of his drawing ability. The "Pogogate" section features humorous news releases written by Kelly in 1952 when Pogo was riding the crest of incredible popularity on college campuses. Numerous Pogo special promotional drawings are reprinted and show both Kelly's skill as an artist and ability to have Pogo charm your socks off.

Pogo Even Better offers the reader the proof of why indeed possums do have ten lives.

Bill Crouch, Jr.

Meet POGO
And Porkypine

THEY'LL BOTH be in the heart-warming new comic strip by Walt Kelly

BEGINNING DATE in
NAME OF PAPER

POGO DAILIES FROM 1949

In our first anthology of *Pogo: The Okefenokee Star* magazine the debut of the syndicated Pogo comic strip was reprinted through June 25, 1949.

The Best of Pogo (Simon & Schuster, 1982) also contained Pogo's pre-syndicated appearances in *The New York Star* newspaper from Oct. 4, 1948 through Jan. 28, 1949 when the paper folded.

This section reprints the balance of the 1949 dailies for the very first time. You will notice both Pogo and Albert the Alligator have more prominent noses than in later strips.

The promotional art to the left is from the package used by newspapers to announce the arrival of Pogo.

THROUGH THE SMOKE AN' FLAME — AIN'T NO CHAINS GONE STAY ME FROM MY POINTED ROUNDS — ...OOP, WHAT THIS?

HOLP! HOLP! HOLP!

WHOA IS YOU, MA'M.

WHUP... DAYLIGHT IS BREAKIN'!

DIN'T MEAN TO SHOVE YOU, LADY...LOOKED LIKE NOBODY WAS AT THE HELM.

I ISN'T NO LADY, MR. MAILMAN— SOMEBODY MUST OF WAS SHOVE A BAIT CAN OVER MY HEAD.

WHY, YOU IS CHURCHY LAFEMME MAN, YOU HEAD IS A VERITABLE BAIT MINE.

OH, I IS GOT TALENT!

7-27

H'LO, PORKYPINE. CHURCHY IS WEARIN' BAIT ON HIS HEAD...LOOKS LIKE A LADY.

IT REMINDS ME OF AN ANECDOTE—I WAS TOLD TO MAKE FOLKS LAUGH MORE...

THIS SHOULD CONVULSE YOU... A MAGICIAN SAID TO HIS ASSISTANT—"WHO WAS THAT LADY I SAWED WITH YOU LAST NIGHT?"

WHEE HEE HEE HOOO

NO SENSE OF HUMOR, THEY TELL ME IS THE MARK OF A DULLARD—YOU, SIR, FIT THE BILL. DULLARD, DULLARD, DULLARD!

ONE OF THE BAITY WORMS WINGLED DOWN MY BACK—I GOT GIGGLIN' AN' DIN'T HEAR THE STORY—WHAT HE SAY?

WHO KNOWS...? HE DIN'T FINISH.

7-28

GONE BORRY THIS BOWL AND SPOON, POGO, SO'S I CAN BORRY SOME SUGAR IF I GETS THE LOAN OF SOME COFFEE.

POGO

HEE HEE! YOU FINALLY GETS YOUR BOWL, EH, BOLL WEEVIL?

WELL, OL' BOLL WEEVIL! YOU FINALLY GETS A BOWL—HAW! HAW! HAW!

AAAAAH!

HEE HEE! YOU FINALLY GETS A BOWL, EH, BOLL WEEVIL?

PHOO

HELLO, MR. WEEVIL.

BY JING! THAT'S JEST 'BOUT EE-NUFF IMPERTIMENTS FROM YOU!

7-29

THEY WAS A ANT UNDERNEATH OF THIS BOWL, POGO...HE DONE VANISHED.

HERE HE BE...HE BURROWED OUT.

NOPE! I FROM CHINA.

HAW! CHINA INDEED! WHERE'S YOUR PING TAIL?

US WEARIN' 'EM SHORT THIS YEAR—PARED TO THE HEAD BONE.

LET'S US HEAR A MESS OF CHINA TALK.

WHAT KIND OF CHINA YOU WANTS? MANDARIN, CASTILIAN, WEDGEWOOD?

LISTEN AT THIS: ORANGE PEKOE, EGG FOO YOUNG, NO TICKEE NO SHIRTEE.

GREAT! AMAZIN' AND EDUCATIONAL.

EGG FOO, INDEED.

7-30

— 15 —

Strip 8-1:
YOU ISN'T FROM CHINA --- YOU IS MERE A COMMON ANT BUG.

WHY, MR. WEEVIL, I SEES OUR ORIENTAL FRIEND CLUMB OUTEN THIS HOLE AFORE MY VERY OWN SOFT BROWN EYES.

SHO' 'NUFF... I WILL TALK SOME MO' CHINA: CHICKEN CHOW DOG... EGG FOO YOUNG --- OKAY, BOSS, PLENNY STARCH.

MAN! WHAT MORE PROOF IS YOU NEED--?

WHO CAN'T TALK THAT KIND CHINESE? EGG FOO YOUNG, EGG FOO OLD, EGG FOO IN THE POT NINE DAYS COLD.

THIS HOLE YOU IS SAY COME UP FROM CHINA IS ONLY A INCH DEEP.

AY-MAZIN'! DIN'T HAVE NO IDEA CHINA WAS SO CLOSE!

OH SHO'!

Strip 8-2:
I CLAIM OL' ANT ISN'T REALLY FROM CHINA --- TO PROVE IT, LET'S SEE IF HE KNOW THE CHINESE WEEVIL TRICK.

SHOOT, WEEVIL BOY.

EVER'BODY PUTS HANDS OVER MOUTH AN' SAY: SPEAK NO WEEVIL! HANDS OVER EARS, SAY: HEAR NO WEEVIL!

MOOME MO MOOBLE.

HEAR NO WEEVIL.

NOW THEN, SMARTLY! HANDS OVER EYES --- -- SEE NO WEEVIL!

AN' THEN----?

Strip 8-3:
OL' WEEVIL WAS DOIN' A CHINESE TRICK AN' HE DISAPPEARED, UNFORTUNATE WITH THE LUNCH.

REMINDS ME OF A CASE IN THE BELGIAN CONGO, SIR --- I WHIPPED OUT MY DERRINGER AND SHOT AT ONCE.

AT WUNTZ? WHAT HE DO?

WHAT HE DO? WHO DO?

WUNTZ DO HOO DOO? HOW DO HE DO HOO DOO?

ONCE DO WHO DO? WHAT? WHAT!? TO WIT, WHAT.

YOU SAYS YOU PULLS YOUR GUN AND SHOOT WUNTZ, THE HOO DOO MAN, I SAYS HOW HE DO IT AND YOU SAYS TO WIT --- I'LL TO WIT YOU IN THE NOSE, YOU OL' WINGBAG!

AAARGH-- IF I HAD MY TRUSTY DERRINGER HERE, SIR--

GUESS I GOIN' BACK TO CHINA.

Strip 8-4:
STAND BACK, SON! IT'S A FLEA.

OH- A WOOD FLEA --- NO NEED TO FEAR --- HE SAYS HE'S GOT A STORY TO TELL. VERY FAINT VOICE --- NO NOISE NOW.

HAW! PRETTY GOOD, HUH?

CONFIDENTIALLY, I DON'T BLAME YOU FOR NOT LAUGHING --- I WAS JUST BEING POLITE... HE SHOULD NEVER TRY TO HANDLE DIALECT STORIES.

GREAT! STRING! JUST THE THING FOR A NATURAL BORN NEST.

OOP--TROUBLE!

ROSCOE! YOU IS GONE BALDY UP MISTER PORKY PINE.

YOU'LL GOTTA FORGIVE ROSCOE, PORKY PINE-- HE JES' A PINFEATHER TAD WHAT ISN'T FOUND HIMSELF YET.

I ISN'T EVEN LOOKED FOR ME.

I CAN WELL UNDERSTAND WHY! WHEN HE DOES MAKE THAT FRIGHTENING DISCOVERY HE'LL THROW HIMSELF BACK.

OH, YOU KNOWS IMPETUOUS YOUTH.

THAT'S ME?

POGO, MY BOY! TODAY'S YOUR LUCKY DAY.

WHY, DOCTOR SEMINOLE SAM, THE CARPET BAG MAN! WHAT YOU SELLIN' THIS TIME?

HERE'S A LITTLE ITEM--- A HUMOROUS TALE ENGRAVED ON THE POINT OF A PIN ---- READ IT? PRETTY FUNNY, HUH?!

IT'S A MITE OBSCURE.

THERE'S A TRICK TO IT--- TURN AND BEND OVER -- YOU'LL GET THE POINT-- HAW HAW HAW!

LIKE THIS?

I IS A PORKYPINE BY TRADE AND CAN OUTPOINT YOU IN THAT GAME WITHOUT MUSSIN' MY COIFFURE, SO REE-LAX DOC, REE-LAX!

OH! I BEG YO' PARDON!

8-26

NATURALLY ANYBODY WHO CAN ENGRAVE MESSAGES ON THE POINT OF A PIN MUST BE PRETTY SMALL....SO IN MY LEFT HAND I HOLD THE MICROSCOPIC BUG, NAME OF CURRIER B. IVES, THE FAMOUS ENGRAVER.

CURRIER B. IVES? HMMP-- WHAT'S "B" FOR?

WHAT'S BEFORE? NOTHIN'--'CEPT "MISTER". LOOK QUICK--- HE'S SHY.

"B" FOR "MISTER"? HUMPH.

DIN'T SEE NOTHIN'.

BEFORE "MISTER"? THERE'S NOTHING BEFORE "MISTER" NOTHING BUT SPACE-- SPACE AND AIR.

UNDOUBTABLE YOU MEANS WELL, SIR, BUT YOU IS A MITE LOOSE IN THE FLUE.

RESTRAIN YOURSELF. CURRIER-- THO' I KNOW AN INSULT TO ME CURDLES YOUR HEART'S BLOOD!

8-27

WHAT'S ALL THE FUSS?

OL' DOC SEMINOLE SAM, THE CARPET BAG MAN, IS GOT A BUG NAME OF CURRIER B. IVES WHAT ENGRAVES FUNNY STORIES ON THE POINT OF A PIN.

SINCE ONLY YOU CAN SEE MR. IVES OR READ THE JOKES, PRAY READ OFF A BIT, DOC.

VERY WELL.

IT SAY HERE: "THE MAXIMUM INCLINATION OF THE PLANE OF A NAVIGATIONAL PLANET TO THE PLANE OF THE ELIPTIC IS THREE DEGREES." ------HMMMM!

GENTLEMEN, APPARENTLY I'VE MIXED THE PINS. THIS ONE SEEMS TO BEAR THE CONSTITUTION OF A SMALL SOUTHERN REPUBLIC IN A FOREIGN TONGUE.

GO AHEAD AN' FINISH HER-SHE STARTS OUT FUNNY.

10-24

POGO IS TURNED UP MISSIN'! AS GAME WARDEN I IS GAME AS THEY COME --- GOTTA FIND THE BOY!

HOLD ON 'ARF A MO', GUVNOR-- INSPECTOR BEAUREGARD DETECTS A FOOTPRINT.

AS GAME WARDEN, I SAYS BULLY FOR YOU, DEPUTY BEAUREGARD.

SNUFF-NIFFLE- MFUMPH-- SNOOF SNIFF.

A MYSTERIOUS TRAIL-- AS EVIL-ODORED A SET OF PRINTS AS I'VE SNIFFED IN A LONG DISTINGUISHED CAREER OF CRIMINOLOGY.

AS GAME WARDEN, I SAYS: ON, ON, ON! FIND POGO!

10-25

NOW'S MY CHANCE TO ESCAPE WHILE OL' FOX AN' WILEY CAT IS SLEEPIN' OFF THAT RUBBER BOOT THEY ATE.

IS I ASLEEP OR IS OUR POT WALKIN' AWAY?

IT'S WORTH A POT SHOT JUS' IN CASE WE ISN'T WATCHIN' THE SAME DREAM.

POW!

BWANG!

SOMEBODY THINKIN' OF ME --- MY EARS RINGIN' LIKE A BARREL-HOUSE BANG-JO.

10-26

THE KEEN EYE OF THE DOG, MAN'S BEST FRIEND, FASTENS ON A SUSPICIOUS FUGITIVE.

HOLD ON! YOU TURTLES IS GETTIN' TOO RECKLESS-- CHARGIN' 'ROUN' THE SWAMP!

ALBERT! I ISN'T NO TURTLE --- I IS ME, POGO POSSUM.

POSSUMS DON'T HAVE SHELLS THE WAY YOU TURTLES DO, SON.

BUT I IS STUCK!

YOU SHO' IS STUCK! YOU IS RUN UP AGIN THE LAW, TURTLE!

10-27

US HUNTERS THANKS YOU, GAME WARDEN, FOR STOPPIN' OUR DUCK WHAT WE CAUGHT.

DUCK? I THOUGHT HE WERE A TURTLE. NEVER SAW A DUCK WITH ITS SHELL ON.

AS GAME WARDEN I'LL LOOK UP THE RULES --- LET'S SEE---

GAMES FOR ALL OCCASIONS
RULES FOR PINOCHLE MAHJONG ONE O' CAT - HOP SCOTCH - RUSSIAN ROULETTE - ETC.

BY JING, IF I HAD MY SPECKLE TICKLES, I'D READ THIS --- LOOKS INTERESTIN'-

GAMES FOR ALL OCCASIONS

SINCE THE RULES DON'T COVER THE SITUATION, I WILL----DID YOU CATCH THE CRITTUR FAIR AND SQUARE?

I CAUGHT HIM FAIR AN' SQUARE ON THE MUSH WITH A IRON POT.

WALT KELLY

YOU SAY YOU GONE *EAT* THIS DUCK YOU CAUGHT--- BUT HE SAY HE IS POGO POSSUM--- I SAY HE'S A TURTLE--- SHOULD I 'WARD YOU THE CRITTUR?... AS GAME WARDEN I WANTS TO 'WARD FAIR AN' SQUARE--

MY FRIEND, I COULDN'T DISAGREE WITH YOU LESS-- I DON'T WANT TO INFLUENCE YOU, *BUT* SOON AS WE HAS A FIRE --------

WE'LL COOK UP THAT DUCK AND *YOU* IS MARKED DOWN FOR A VERY SMART, CHOICE PORTION.

AS GAME WARDEN I SAYS LET'S BUILD THE FIRE RIGHT OVER HERE BY THE OL' OAK.

10-28

HONEST, I ISN'T A DUCK OR TURTLE, --- I IS MERE ME, POGO.

SO LONG AS YOU IS TENDER, SON, I ISN'T PARTICKLISH.

THE DUCK RECIPE IS TOO HARD TO READ ---- FIGGER THE QUARRY IS A OYSTER? OYSTER RECIPE IS GOT EASIER WORDS IN HER.

SHO' NUFF-- SHOOT.

"ROUST TH' CRITTUR OUTEN HIS SHELL", IT SAY --SEE! HE IN A SHELL SO HE A OYSTER --- NEXT IT SAY, "IN MONTHS WITHOUT ANY 'R' IN 'EM, OYSTERS IS *DEATH!*"

GOLLY-- ANYBODY KNOW WHAT MONTH IT IS?

NOT ME.

NOPE.

JUNE!

10-29

LET'S SHAKE THE CRITTUR OUT OF HIS SHELL.

THEN WE SEE IF YOU GOT A RIGHT TO EAT HIM.

WHY THEM BURGLARS WAS DEECEIVIN' ME --- YOU *IS* POGO, MY BOSOM BUDDY, POGO.

AW, SHECKS-- NATURAL I IS.

CHOOSE YO' WEAPONS, YOU VARMINTS! I GONE WHOP YOU BOTH!

UH- WE FIGHTS WITH KNIVES-- SO KEERFUL!

I FIGHTS WITH A KNIFE *AN'* FORK, AN I IS *HONGRY.*

10-31

FOR THE BENEFIT OF THOSE OF YOU WHO HAVEN'T BEEN PAYIN' ATTENTION, HERE'S THE STORY UP 'TIL NOW.

THIS GONE TAKE A LI'L' TIME --- SO I BRUNG A SAN'WITCH --- SIT DOWN.

NOW FIRST OF ALL--- MMMPH --- THERE WUMS A BOBBLE MOOMP!

SO - GOBF - WHEN WOBBER AN' BOGGO MUMF AROOMMPH SCMBLSH!

THEN ---- MLFGOB GLF - HAW WOBS GOOLLOP - HUG ROTKSPLK.

WELL, THAT'S ABOUT ALL --- MY SAKES, HERE'S THE END OF THE STRIP, ALREADY--- GOODY!

11-1

11-2

H'LO, PORKYPINE. HEAR 'BOUT POGO? OL' FOX AN' OL' CAT TRIED TO *EAT* HIM.

SOME PEOPLE WILL EAT *ANYTHING.*

US RACKETY-COONS IS REE-FINED---- US WASHES THINGS BEFORE US EATS 'EM.

POPPA!

WALT KELLY

11-3

WHY COME IS ONE CRITTUR OR OTHER ALLUS TRYIN' TO EAT SOME OTHER CRITTUR OR ANOTHER, UNCLE PORKY?

'CAUSE CRITTURS GITS HUNGRY-- JES' LIKE FOLKS.

WORM GITS ATE BY FISH AN' FISH GITS ATE BY US, RIGHT?

RIGHT----- SOMEBODY *ALLUS* IS A-EATIN' SOMEBODY.

IN A *PER*FECTLY *FRIEND*LY WAY, NATURAL.

OH, NATURAL.

WALT KELLY

GONNA VISIT OL' POGO AN' CHEER HIM UP?---- HERE'S A STORY TO TELL: *THE WOLF IS A QL' IGNORANT CRITTUR 'CAUSE THE CLOSEST HE EVER GOT TO EDUCATION WAS THE TIME HE ATE RED RIDING HOODS GRAMMAR.*

HAW HAW?

MM - BZZ - WOLF- IGNORANT ----ZMF--- RED RIDING HOOD. ---MM - HUM HMMPH!

WON'T TELL IT----POGO WOULD ONLY FEEL SORRY FOR THE POOR OL' LADY.

POGO

WALT KELLY

11-5

I HEAR YOU WAS ALMOST EATEN BY OL' FOX, SEMINOLE SAM, AND WILEY CAT, AN' NOW YOU IS RESTIN' UP---- I IS HERE TO CHEER YOU UP, POGO.

GOOD! SET DOWN, PORKY.

WE NEVER KNOW WHO'S NEXT.

NOSSIR.

HOPE YOU IS CHEERED... WANT YOU TO KNOW IF I WAS THERE AN' THEY COOKED YOU, I WOULD NOT OF EATEN ANY. GOOD DAY.

THANK YOU, PORKYPINE.

WALT KELLY

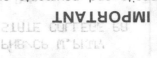

The Land of the Elephant Squash

A Biography of Walt Kelly

Walt Kelly

The first two years of Walt Kelly's life was spent in idleness. This statement is not to be confused with the statement: The first two years of Walt Kelly's life were spent in Philadelphia. Both are true but the first is regrettable and the second is not. If a man must squander his youth, it can be done in Philadelphia with dignity and thrift.

At the age of two, Kelly, his mother, sister and a bag of animal crackers took a train to Bridgeport, Connecticut. At Bridgeport, to hear Kelly tell it, his father was building (single handed) the Remington Arms Munition Plant. It was 1915.

Philadelphia recently paid tribute to the young man's early withdrawal by being the first city outside of New York to print his POGO strip. But in Bridgeport, the boy artist overstayed his welcome. He spent twenty years or more there. Bridgeport has maintained a well-mannered aloofness; Bridgeport KNOWS Kelly and, while it nods continually as it sits on the banks of the Pequonnock river, it never nods at Kelly.

At Hall grammar school he fell madly in love with a dark-eyed young thing, while scarcely through his pablum . . . but when she flunked him in Number Work I, the romance was shattered. This good woman taught the lad how to draw an apple, however, and possibly she marks his first gay mad contact with the world of art and love. It is worth recording that while Kelly DREW apples, other students BROUGHT apples. Kelly was the only scholar to flunk Number Work I twice in a row.

With an audible sigh of relief, the grammar school authorities handed the fledgling artist his diploma. With averted eyes they waited while he crept into the high school (under cover of night) and then hastily locked the doors of the brick building where he had first had knowledge thrust upon him. This was in 1926 and it is significant that in this year the grammar school had a steel wire fence erected.

Warren Harding High School in Bridgeport had a fine student paper and a fine yearbook. Under the impression that he was taking Algebra One, Kelly did a great deal of artwork for both publications.

Foreign languages interested the young man very much. The French class was bulging with pretty girls. Kelly spent three years there.

Graduation from high school revealed that Kelly had been an associate editor of the school paper, a writer of poetry, a cartoonist, a member of the glee club and the only man in the Senior Class who could take apart a ukulele blindfolded. No useful purpose has ever been discovered for blindfolding a uklele (they are not skittish like horses), but the information is there — so we set it down.

Thus armed to the teeth with accomplishment the boy wonder went in search of a job. He exhibited his ukulele, his poems, his editorial finesse, his drawing ability to all who would hold still, and wound up with a job wrapping scrap cloth in a factory that manufactured undergarments for ladies. Word got around that he was good with a brush . . . so he was allowed to sweep out the loft on Saturday afternoons.

An electrical appliance manufacturer did not exactly beckon next, but there was a job smashing faulty switches to be filled and Kelly was out of a job.

Kelly next drifted into newspaper work, a bit of drifting that will demonstrate to anybody that his moorings were really loose, "We can't pay much money, but you'll meet a lot of important people." they said, and Kelly took the job, apparently convinced that the important people would invite him home to dinner six or seven times a week. This hungry state of affairs went on for some time . . . the Front Page Flash of Bridgeport was invited to dinner once in four years and then only by a rival newspaper. Rival newspapers in Bridgeport do not now exist, the opposition having starved to death . . . so it will be seen that this particular night-out was slim but full of gay laughter.

After a number of years of reporting, it was recalled by the Obit man that Kelly had done some drawing for the paper while a mere youth of thirteen. A pen was thrust into his hand and for two long years and an extra five per week he drew and redrew daily strips based on the life of P. T. Barnum, another heroic figure in Bridgeport life. Needless to say, his reporting chores went on. He got a lot of experience at this time, also all the free copies of the paper that he could hide under his coat and all the ink he could use.

Every time the writer got P. T. Barnum to the death bed, old P. T. would get a flash and his entire life would pass again before his eyes to the tune of six months' additional copy. Nothing that Barnum exhibited ever equalled the Colossal Resurrectional Process exhibited by Kelly and the writer. During this spell Kelly drew some political cartoons endorsing the perennial socialist candidate, Jasper McLevy. Jasper was elected mayor and shortly thereafter Kelly left newspaper work. He was frisked for extra copies of the day's edition as he left the ivory tower.

Followed then a short spell of perhaps a year serving as a Department of Public Welfare inspector, investigator, clerk and buffoon to the public.

After a short engagement as a clerk in an art store, most of which time was spent hunting rats in the cellar, Kelly left Bridgeport to starve quietly in New York as a free lance artist. There he could not even catch rats.

With an empty stomach and purse to match, the Voyageur headed for California, reputedly a public garden spot full of breadfruit and plum. The Disney Studios offered shelter there and it was not long before Kelly was the envy of every one of the apprentices as the only man in the crowd with two shirts. (He had found one stuffed into a desk as a dust cloth.)

From this point forward Kelly acquired worldly goods in rapid order. He acquired a wife, who came equipped with an automobile. He acquired a desk calendar which told him the date, 1937. And after a few years he had acquired sufficient knowledge of animation and story work so that he could look busy at the drop of a strange footfall outside his studio door. In a place where the traffic-boys had the regal bearing of Roxy Ushers and the Real Authorities looked like bit players in Keystone Kop Komedies, one had to have an unerring eye.

In these years Kelly made the acquaintance of Walt Disney himself. Disney showed Kelly many tricks . . . not the least of which was the art of sauntering unconcernedly through the gate when one had taken two hours for lunch.

In all fairness to Kelly, it must be admitted that he left of his own accord . . . through a picket line . . . and headed back to New York with his coat tails smoking. Through Walt D., he met up with a book printing firm in the east and set about drawing Comic Books.

He read with growing horror the kinds of comic books being left about where children could reach them, and decided that real juvenile work was his forte, rather than the adventure type of business. "It was impossible for me to draw a naked woman," he explains. "It was blinding work. I would no sooner have her clothes off than I would remove my hat, out of respect. With my eyes unshaded I couldn't see what I was doing. Besides, the editor said that as an adventure man, I had better stick to drawing mice. So I concentrated on puppies, kittens, mice and elves . . . every once in a while glancing back at the men who were grimly penciling out the Pueriles of Pauline . . . taking clothes off and dagging people with butcher knives."

In about 1942 Kelly conceived (some say filched) the idea of a comic feature built around the Southern Swamplands. Retiring to the downstairs bar, he plunged into consideration of this job and was not seen for several days.

The Swampland Feature concerned the doings of a little colored boy named Bumbazine. As side characters there were rabbits, mice, squirrels, lunches, catfish, hollow logs, birds, turtles, an alligator and a 'possum.

The Alligator turned out to be an interesting character, and he was named Albert. Then for a while he shared top billing with Bumbazine. However, Kelly felt there was a chance for people to feel offended at the use of the little boy despite how careful he might be to draw the child attractively — So poor little Bumbazine was put out of a job. His characteristics, i.e.: innocence, naivete, friendliness and sturdy dependability, were taken over by a 'possum who had been playing one day stands in the background. The 'possum was named Pogo and he seems to have lived up to the demands of his role pretty well.

The Feature appeared then at last as "Pogo" in the New York Star after some years of lying fallow. The fan mail convinced the editors that either "Pogo" was popular or Kelly was very busy writing letters. Shortly after the Presidential Campaign of 1948, the New York Star ground to a halt . . . the carpetbaggers leapt from the smoking windows and with them went Kelly, bearing in his arms the infant "Pogo".

Wandering about aimlessly on the sidewalk at the time was a street vendor named Robert M. Hall. As luck would have it Kelly landed directly in Hall's arms, and Hall, taking one look at Pogo, Albert, Walt Kelly and the other animals in the strip struck Kelly smartly across the skull with an iron-bound contract. "Pogo" then went into the syndicate business and Hall followed him in, leaving his push cart to Kelly.

There is not much more to the Kelly story. It was remarked to him the other day that the old desk calendar he'd swiped at Disney's studio was about used up. "You've used all the pages," it was pointed out, "and besides it isn't 1937 anymore."

An incredulous look came into Kelly's eyes, "A new year? Well, what do you know about that?"

"Sure, and besides, 1937 was over thirteen years ago . . . . ."

"Boy," said Kelly, "that 1937 was one loooooong year, wasn't it. You know I *thought* it was running a little overtime."

So we leave beautiful POGO POGO, the land of the Elephant Squash, and steer our ship back through the sunset waters to the beautiful strains of 'Possum up a Gum Stump, Coonie's in the Holler."

* * *

APPENDIX

Kelly himself is a rather imposingly flabby man of some thirty-six winters. He is the oldest boy-artist in the country . . . a title which he will defend at any time. He is married to

Helen, a well-balanced young woman who maintains that position by ignoring Kelly completely. They have three children,

Kathleen, aged seven, who plays the piano, draws better than her father and always could add better than he . . . . .

Carolyn, aged four-and-a-half, an artist of great promise who has a carefree nature that makes her a poor risk to be in charge of the roller coaster . . . . .

Peter, aged two-and-a-half, a man with a mechanical turn of mind, who can already spell words like HORSE, giving them his own pronunciation. Horse is FORCE . . . Story is Downy . . . A reckless man with a truck.

They live in Darien, Connecticut, in a house held together by paint and inertia . . . inasmuch as the paint is rapidly flaking away, the place is becoming a death trap and Kelly hopes to abandon it some dark night when no one is looking.

Kelly's mother and father live in Stratford, Connecticut, near the Housatonic river. Their windows afford a clear view of the road so that at the appearance of Kelly they can slip out the back door and nip into a boat.

Kelly works at home, a condition that bothers him a little because his wife makes so much noise shoveling coal and shaking down the furnace. Days when she's out chopping wood behind the house, Kelly says, are much better.

He writes his own material by scribbling on table cloths . . . roughs it out in blue pencil, letters it, and then inks the drawings. His wife is running out of table cloths. He gets enough fan mail so that it is hard for him to answer it. Big globs of it hang around until it gets in the way of the food. Then somebody does something about it.

"Pogo" is the first strip Walt Kelly ever attempted seriously. Like a great many other people he had thought of the strip he would draw some day or the book he would write or the horse he would win on . . . His wife keeps thinking of book cases he would build.

He says *Pogo* is the warm hearted little guy we all would like to think we are. *Albert* is closer to what we think of the other fellow. Kelly points out that, as an old hand at being the "other fellow", he's pretty sure that Albert comes close to being an average American male. Always full of knowledge and gusto that backfires . . . deep down the Alligator is warm hearted and generous, but he doesn't really like to let anybody know it for fear they'll think he's soft.

KELLY'S LIFE OF P.T. BARNUM

In Ten Ever-Lovin' Blue-Eyed Years with Pogo, *Walt Kelly wrote about his youthful adventure illustrating the life of P.T. Barnum; however none of his illustrations have been reprinted before. The Introduction is by Kelly reprinted from* Ten Ever-Lovin'.

THE emergence of **P. T. Bridgeport** marked the second time that the lettering in the balloons was so styled as to indicate the tone of voice of the character. I was brought up in Bridgeport, and whereas Bridgeport had nodded on the banks of the Pequonnock for many years, it never nodded at me. When I left I carried, besides a few cucumbers and an extra shoe, memories of the days when Bridgeport was the great Circus Town. Not that I had lived through it all; I would have to be 196 years old, more or less, and, despite what a few friends think, I am not half that. But Barnum was the patron saint of Bridgeport. I know. I illustrated his life three times running for the Bridgeport *Post* when I worked there for a few bowls of whey. I started running the last time the thing appeared.

Barnum had one third as many lives as a cat, according to Charlie Greene, the writer, and according to the willing editors of the *Post*. Charlie (who weighed about as much as a polar bear) and I became great friends. He was perhaps 50 years my senior, had been a postmaster, and was an authority on the harbors and rivers of southern Connecticut. He wrote about them a lot and was fond of saying he was the outlet for the inlets. Besides that, he was an authority on P. T. Barnum and nothing made him beam across a piece of custard pie quite

THE COMING OF TOM THUMB

When Barnum was 35 years of age he was to attempt a feat of showmanship probably never equalled before or since, a feat that was to bring him a shower of gold. Far from his own fondest hopes the wealthiest people of the world opened their purses to be entertained by two Connecticut Yankees; one a full grown man and the other a personality who could conceal his body under a bushel measure with ease. General Tom Thumb had a brain that was brilliant and was a natural thespian. Less than two feet tall, perfectly formed, rosy cheeks and curly brown hair, the ladies of the courts of Europe's royal courts raved about the dear little man. What royalty patronized the mobs crowded to see. A dwarf born in Bridgeport became the most famous midget of all time.

In 1842 P.T. Barnum was in Albany during the month of November on business. The Hudson River was frozen over and no boats were running to New York. Barnum crossed country until he struck the Housatonic railroad and came to Bridgeport over it. His brother, Philo F. Barnum, kept the leading hotel, the Franklin, here, and that night after supper the Barnum brothers sat down in the hotel office for a chat about things in general. Incidentally Philo told Phineas that there was a little boy in town whose body had not grown since he was six months old but who was perfectly formed and in good health, and as bright as a diamond. Museum owner Barnum decided to stay over the next day and the brother had the little boy brought to the hotel by his parents. The boy was Charles S. Stratton and his parents were Mr. and Mrs. Sherwood E. Stratton.

It was no easy task for the showman to induce the parents to enter into an agreement to place their child on display but Mr. Barnum succeeded, as he usually did, in getting people interested in his plan, and the Strattons decided to enter into the enterprise for a short time. It was agreed that the boy and his mother should come to New York for four weeks with all expenses paid and compensation of $3 per week. Thanksgiving Day fell on December 8 in 1842 and on that day Tom Thumb made his debut at the American museum. Imagine Mrs. Stratton's surprise when she saw the words "General Tom Thumb from England" emblazoned over a huge banner in front of the museum and the announcement that he was 11 years of age instead of five. But the first appearances were for brief periods only and no strain was placed upon the tiny mite who was to be educated as a showman by the king of showmen.

Barnum knew the power of contrast. He called the atom of humanity a general and uniformed him as such. He took great pains to educate the diminutive prodigy in grace and deportment and with a knowledge of history and current events so that the questions he answered correctly appeared stupendous coming from so small a brain and the lips of a mere baby. The native talent of "Charley" Stratton was marvelous and he had a keen sense of the ludicrous. As an attraction he was worth many times his weight in gold. Heralded as English the American fancy for European exotics made him a great public favorite. At the end of the four weeks he was engaged for one year at $7 per week with a $50 gratuity at the end of the year and all expenses for himself and mother. Barnum had the right to exhibit Tom Thumb anywhere in the United States.

THE MONEY BEGINS TO COME IN

Barnum was nearing his goal—Buckingham Palace and the royal family as the hosts to the little baby midget whose wit and brilliance had increased amazingly. To the showman's great delight he received an invitation from the wife of the then richest man in the world. Baroness Rothschild. Barnum and the general spent two hours in her sumptuous drawing room with a party of a score of ladies and gentlemen. They came away with a purse filled with gold. The shower of gold had begun.

Piccadilly was the center of fashion and "Egyptian Hall" was a famous center for the wealthy. Barnum engaged it and commenced to hold a series of afternoon levees there which were attended by throngs of the wealthy people who wanted to satisfy their curiosity by meeting the little general. Barnum made the exhibition unique and the winsome little general with the apparent wisdom of a sage became a stellar attraction.

like the hazarded opinion, induced by bad glasses and worse coffee, that he looked a lot like Barnum himself. He did indeed look like the Barnum that I drew. There was no good copy on Barnum around the office. I won't say that our morgue was bare, but the mice had to fight out in the open. Neither will I go so far as to suggest that Charlie made up part of Barnum's life. However, it was pretty interesting stuff. The more I drew pictures of Barnum, the more they looked like Charlie Greene. Charlie, a real-estate reporter among other things, died a few years ago and I half expected to see his obit illustrated by the life of P. T.

After the "Egyptian Hall" exhibitions had continued for several weeks Barnum received an invitation to breakfast with Minister Everett and here he was introduced to Charles Murray, an author and writer who asked Barnum as to his plans. Barnum replied that he was going to France but would be glad to remain if there was any possibility of securing an interview with the Queen. Mr. Murray kindly offered his good offices in the case.

The next morning one of the queen's lifeguards in resplendent uniform appeared at the Tom Thumb mansion at Grafton and Bond streets bringing a note conveying the queen's invitation to General Tom Thumb and his guardian, Mr. Barnum to appear at Buckingham palace on the evening specified. On the same day Mr. Murray gave the queen's command to suffer the midget to appear as he would anywhere else without training in the use of titles and etiquette. Victoria wanted Tom to be natural and without restraint.

While visiting at the royal palace Barnum learned that the gentleman in waiting who had charge of the "Court Journal" was in the palace at the time and anxious that the publication should contain more than a line. Barnum asked to see him. The result was that the showman obtained quite a good sized notice in the Palace publication.

Barnum was obliged after the Palace visit to secure a larger hall in London, so great was the eagerness of the populace to see the midget who had become the fashion. The little idea of Philo and Phineas Barnum hatched out in the old Franklin hotel in Bridgeport had the greatest city in the world agog. General Tom Thumb was the fashion.

Queen Victoria sent a second command for the little general to come to the palace that he might talk with the prince of Wales. Tom Thumb shook hands with the prince and said: "The prince is taller than I am but I feel as big as anybody," and proceeded to strut about as though inches were really feet. Several small pieces of furniture had been sent to the palace Yellow Room by Barnum and the general escorted the little princess royal to a seat beside him on a sofa.

The Queen of the Belgians was a guest at Buckingham. She was the daughter of King Louis Philippe, the then ruler of the kingdom of France. She asked the little general where he was going after he left London. "Paris," was the reply of Tom Thumb and the queen said that her father would surely be pleased to welcome him. On a third visit to see the children of the royal family Leopold, King of the Belgians asked Tom Thumb what song he liked best. "Yankee Doodle," was the quick reply.

The great showman who was a friend of Lincoln also felt at home in the presence of kings. While he was in France, King Louis Philippe, the citizen king, was on the throne.

Jumbo, probably the most famous and best loved elephant whose name is a word of common usage in the English language, was famous before Mr. Barnum brought him to this country.

Louis Philippe had been in America and roughed it in the West. Having a high regard for Americans he treated little "General Tom Pouce" like an ambassador and presented him with a large emerald brooch set with diamonds.

Early in 1861 an English traveler met a party of Hamran Arabs. They had in their possession a baby elephant that was to be floated down a river on a raft in hopes that an advantageous sale might be made to someone at a city.

The French monarch was so condescending that Barnum asked him directly for permission to have Tom Thumb's tiny coach in the famous Longchamps celebration for display at court and among the fashionable equipages that would be that day on the Champs Elysees. "Call on the prefect of police and you will find a permit ready for you," said the king graciously.

As a baby Jumbo was small and had the Arabs known that they possessed a youngster that was to become the second largest, if not the largest, pachyderm known to man he would probably have stayed with them. Although African elephants are accredited with being ill tempered, Jumbo was destined to be the pampered pet of the children of London for several years.

Jumbo, who might have been humiliated if he had known he was traded for a snorting, near-sighted rhinoceros, settled down to what would have been a very commonplace routine for any ordinary elephant in the London Zoological Society. But he had a personality and began to be friendly with children who visited the zoo.

Queen Victoria heard about the elephant which seemed to enjoy big loads of kiddies on its back and she paid it a visit so the Royal children could have a ride.

From 1865 to 1882 he became the pampered and petted favorite of the zoo. He grew rapidly and his friendliness increased with his size. He was trusted to carry whole bevies of children on his back. His understanding, gentleness and intelligence exceeded that of the average elephant.

But Jumbo continued to grow and his size made the management of the zoo fearful that he might take on the peculiar characteristics of other African elephants, and in such a case an ordinary sized elephant would be hard enough to handle.

"Scotty," his keeper, who hardly ever left the creature for an hour shared even half his ale and porter, and sometimes a little hard liquor with Jumbo. The big elephant liked his schnapps, but never over indulged. "Scotty" maintained that a little whisky was good for a stranger to London fogs.

The wary directors foresaw that the big animal would cause havoc if he should go on a rampage and take it in his head to visit Piccadilly Square. In America there was a showman who knew Jumbo, and trusted him.

CHILDREN OBJECT TO SALE

It was with great despair the children of London who flocked to the London zoo to ride on his back, heard that the zoo directors contemplated selling their massive friend for the sum of $10,000. He was so kind to them that they felt the talk of his becoming unmanageable was without warrant.

Officers of the society little dreamed of the storm of protest that would follow what they thought was a profitable escape from the dread of having a wild elephant upon their hands.

As soon as it became known that Jumbo had been sold there were protests from all classes from the throne down to the humblest Londoner and the press of Germany, France and the United States. The New Herald said a war between America and England was imminent if Barnum took the British children's pet.

BARNUM REMAINS FIRM

Barnum sealed the fate of Jumbo. He cabled the editor of the London Daily Telegraph sending his compliments to the British nation and said: "Fifty millions of American citizens anxiously awaiting Jumbo's arrival. My 40 years invariable practice of exhibiting best can procure make's Jumbo's presence here imperative."

"Hundred thousand pounds would be no inducement to cancel the purchase. In December intend to visit Australia in person with Jumbo and entire mammoth combination of seven shows via California thence through Suez Canal. Following summer in London. Shall exhibit in every large city of Great Britain."

"May afterwards return Jumbo to old position in Royal Zoological Gardens. Wishing long life to the British nation, the Daily Telegraph and Jumbo, I am the public's obedient servant, P. T. Barnum." London mourned what was termed the foolish bargain of Royal Zoological Council.

JUMBO STARTS FOR U.S.

While all London kept up its entreaties to keep Jumbo in London Mr. Barnum commenced his preparations to have the amiable monster sent to America. The superintendent of the Society of Cruelty to Animals in London watched for an opportunity to build a legal wall that the elephant could not be taken over.

When the Assyrian Monarch sailed out of the Thames thousands collected on the banks of the river, on boats and on buildings to get a last glimpse if possible of the famous Jumbo, but he was safely below decks in the huge crate.

The day was saved by old "Scotty" the keeper who learning that Jumbo was sure to go said that he would go along with the creature with which he shared his apples, his sugar, his whiskey and his ale.

Jumbo had a rough 15 days passage across the Atlantic. The elephant was never left alone. When "Scotty" the keeper slept Barnum's chief elephant man. Neuman. was present and the animal was never in darkness. Jumbo was seasick for two or three days, but proved a good sailor at the end of the voyage.

It was "Scotty" who lured Jumbo into a huge crate. Once inside the animal put up a terrific struggle. Quieted down by the soothing words of the keeper from without the big animal in the huge container was hoisted on a lighter and taken alongside the S.S. Assyrian Monarch, lying at anchor in the Thames. Once aboard Jumbo was bound for New York.

A great crowd awaited Jumbo in New York where he was unloaded in his crate to a lighter in the lower bay. Put ashore at the Battery, wheels were put under the crate and eight horses pulled Jumbo to Madison Square Garden where the circus was showing. It had cost $30,000 to get Jumbo to America.

JUMBO — THE CHILDREN'S FRIEND

Arriving at Madison Square Garden it was discovered that while the doors of the big theater might admit Jumbo they would not admit the crate that held the giant elephant. Covered with blankets and tarpaulins the former popular member of Her Majesty's zoo slept in the streets of New York.

Barnum had guessed right, the drawing powers of the great elephant were not only in his great frame but at the box office. The first ten days' receipts fully reimbursed the great showman for his $30,000 expenditure.

Until he died Jumbo was a great income producer. English children kept up their interest in him. Vast quantities of letters arrived addressed to Mr. Jumbo, and many small packages of dainties. No animal ever held the friendships of children the way Jumbo did. Several packages were simply addressed "Mr. Jumbo, New York, U.S.A."

JUMBO DIES A HERO

Mr. Barnum looked forward to the day that he would send Jumbo back to the children of London. The big creature was an attraction on the road with the circus and was a patient traveler. Children in all the big cities were given the opportunity to ride on his back.

Jumbo never developed the trouble with his disposition that the London zoological authorities looked for, and if anything he became more docile. Besides liking children of human beings he became attached to the baby elephant that was with the big circus.

On the morning of September 13, 1885 when the Barnum circus was in St. Thomas, Canada, Jumbo was struck by an express train and killed. "Scotty" the old keeper, said that Jumbo charged the oncoming locomotive to protect the baby elephant.

Day Time

KELLY FANTASY ARTWORK

After Walt Kelly left Disney Studios he did numerous illustrations of fantasy and children's stories. He also illustrated an entire book of Mother Goose. Most of his fantasy artwork has never been reprinted and these drawings give us a rare glimpse of his talent in that area.

Night Time

A dumpety pointy sort of somebody sitting calm and comfortable on the top step . . .

They rested behind a cloud

Walt Kelly's
Mother Goose

PEASE PORRIDGE HOT

Pease porridge hot.
Pease porridge cold.
Pease porridge in the pot
Nine days old.

Some like it hot,
Some like it cold.
Some like it in the pot
Nine days old.

LITTLE BO PEEP

Little Bo Peep has lost her sheep,
And doesn't know where to find them.
Leave them alone and they'll be home,
Wagging their tails behind them.

The Pogofenokee Swamp

Written especially for *Okefenokee Star* readers.

By POGO

IN 1943 I was born, not in the real Okefenokee Swamp, but in a comic book. (The real Okefenokee Swamp is a wildlife wilderness, 30x40 miles, in southeastern Georgia and northeastern Florida.) At that time I played only a bit part. The leading character was a little boy. And next to him there was an alligator whose name was Albert. In those days Albert Alligator was ferocious and a braggart. He was always boasting about the things he was going to do. He never did any of them. He tried, though. I am very glad he didn't succeed because one of the things he wanted to do was quite distasteful to me. Albert wanted to eat me.

Maybe that's why I looked so sad in those days.

Later it seemed to Mr. Walt Kelly, the boss, that the boy slowed us animals down. "Animals are much more sensible and a lot more fun to work with," said Mr. Kelly, and he threw the little boy out—gently. Then when the animals in *Pogo* talked to each other, it made more sense. Animals do not really say anything much to humans, or in front of humans either. "It doesn't pay to let them know too much," says Mr. Rackety Coon.

When the little boy had gone off, Albert turned out to be a real friend to the other animals in Okefenokee

1969

1943

Swamp. He was still very grumpy, though, and still acting ferocious when he felt like it; and he was still boasting. Every once in a while, even now, he swallows somebody by mistake. Spelunkers (people who explore caves) then go in and rescue the poor lost soul. Albert does not do this very often, because spelunkers are apt to light matches and to carry torches around in your insides in case you've swallowed anybody. Very uncomfortable. "It gives me heart-burn," says Albert, "and then stomach-burn and then liver-burn."

We all lived in the comic-book swamp until about 1947. Mr. Kelly went to work then for a newspaper in New York City, and in 1948 he made a comic strip out of our adventures. The first thing Albert did was to swallow a pollywog child. It took two months to get the poor little beast out of there.

Exactly twenty years ago, May 1949 to be exact, Albert Alligator and I started our first work in national syndication. That means that in strip form, we were sent off to newspapers all around the country

CHURCHY & HOWLAND

where we appeared every day on the comics page. This takes a lot of work. Mr. Kelly makes the drawings, and then they are engraved. The plates or engravings are then impressed on a matrix—on many matrices, in fact. A matrix is a lightweight asbestos paperboard mold into which melted zinc can be poured to make a printing plate. This is done at each of the newspapers so that the drawings can be printed in every city.

Along the way we had gathered many friends in the swamp. Churchy La Femme is a turtle by trade. Howland Owl is a scientific type, who pretends to be very knowledgeable. Beauregard Bugleboy Frontenac, a

hound-dog, came into the swamp looking for someone who was lost. It turned out to be him. Porkypine is a gruff little philosopher with a heart bigger than he is. Bun Rabbit, a virtuoso drummer, likes to collect holidays. The Rackety Coon Chile is sometimes smarter than the adults. And Miss Ma'm'selle Hepzibah, a lady skunk, is much admired.

Besides these special friends, many other people joined our company— bears, snakes, butterflies, worms, and mice. Somebody tried to count them all one time, but gave up after identifying about 150.

Mr. Kelly confesses that each of the characters, good and bad alike, represents a side or two of his own personality, for better or worse. This is why he says that we should not judge the other fellow too harshly. "You may be somewhat like him yourself. Try to understand him."

Bun Rabbit's interest in holidays led to a story that is being adapted for television in animation. I thought that anybody should be allowed to celebrate the holiday of his choice any time he wanted to. So we set about acting that out. The story mainly involves Porkypine and a lot of confusion.

Confusion seems to be a way of life in the Okefenokee Swamp that we live in. We try to do things right but they turn out a little upside down or inside out. So, as Porkypine says, we don't take life too seriously, "because it ain't nohow permanent."

ALBERT

Mr. Walt Kelly draws all the pictures of us Okefenokee folks—this is a picture he drew of him drawing pictures of us.

We call Mr. Kelly the boss, but sometimes we squirm when he is drawing us. Just look at all the pictures he's tossed aside. Actually he's very understanding for a human, and he seems almost like one of us Swamp folks.

Mr. Kelly thinks, and I do too, that you might like to color the pictures after you finish reading our story.

— 67 —

3-8 PUBLISHERS - HALL SYNDICATE INC.

WHAT WE GOTTA DO IS *TAKE* THIS PITTSBURGH TEAM IN TWO STRAIGHT SPRING TRAININ' GAMES.

GET IN THERE AN' *FIGHT!*

FIGHT? I DUNNO; SOME OF THEIR GUYS ARE PERTY *BIG!*

RIGHT! SO WHAT WE'LL DO IS *OUTTHINK* THEM.

WITH *WHAT?*

WHEN WE MEET THE *PITTSBURGH TEAM* IN OUR SPRING SERIES, WE'LL FLASH A *REAL SURPRISE!* CATCH 'EM *TEE*-TOTALLY UNAWARES.

WHAT'LL WE *DO?*

PULL A GUN ON 'EM!

3-19 PUBLISHERS-HALL SYNDICATE INC.

WE'LL *OUTFOX* THEM BY COMING PREPARED FOR *VOLLEYBALL!*

WE'LL SPRING A *LIGHTNING ATTACK!* BEFORE THEY CAN *REE*-COVER, WE'LL BE **100 POINTS** AHEAD!

HOW YOU GONNA *SURPRISE* 'EM?....THEY'LL BE *TIPPED OFF,* IF NOT BY THE *SIZE* OF THE BALL, THEN BY THE *NET* WHEN YOU STRING IT ACROSS THE INFIELD.

THEY'LL *SUSPECT* SOMETHIN', HUH?

IT'S GUYS LIKE YOU SPOILS A LOT OF *NOBLE* EXPERIMENTS.

WELL, *ON* TO THE PITTSBURGHS' TRAININ' CAMP... WE'LL TAKE TWO OUT OF THREE!

OKAY, NOW WHERE IS THESE PIRATES *TRAININ'?* FLORIDA, ARIZONA, CALIFORNIA OR HONOLULU?

UM....I AIN'T GOT A SCHEDULE.

DETAILS DETAILS.

OKEFENOKEE MUDWUMPS

© 1972 WALT KELLY

POGO PRIMER FOR PARENTS

This is a
television
set.

This is a parent...This is another.

This is a child.   This is a parent afraid
of a t.v. set.

The child is not
afraid of the t.v. set.

Why is the parent
afraid of the t.v. set?

He is afraid because of what it might do
to his child.

He thinks it might turn him into a monster.

He thinks it might turn him into an *ungrateful* monster...

.....A monster who will destroy the happy home.

Why, then, does the parent let his child watch t.v.?

Maybe he feels little children should be seen and not heard.

Maybe because he is busy with sports pages. It takes time to find out the editor is wrong about the box score.

Why does the mother parent let her child watch t.v.?

Because the telephone rings and it must be answered.

She must talk to somebody about something important.

She cannot do housework...And have headaches...

And watch children all day...
So she lets the t.v. set watch the children.

This is better than letting the child
get run over by a truck.

This is what parents
are afraid of:

The t.v. set, children,
trucks...

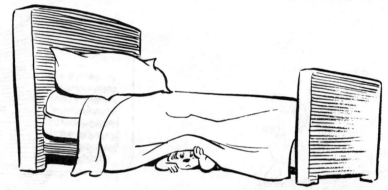

What are little children afraid of?

They are afraid of boredom, also *frustration.*
They want to know what to do...

They are afraid of monsters. On t.v.
they sometimes meet a lot of them.

These monsters can become their
constant companions.

Monsters are not as good as parents
to learn things from.

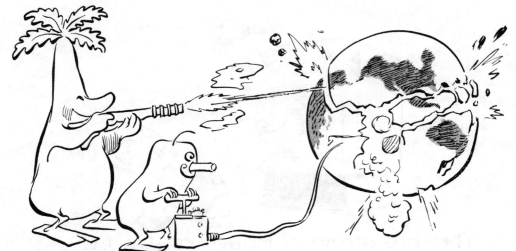

Except in matters of destruction.

What *does* the child want then?

He wants to be *loved*...
He wants guidance... He wants the
parents to share things with him...
Maybe even t.v., radio, comic books, broccoli...

BRAND NEW CHAPTER

These are psychiatrists.
They are very learned men.

They care what happens to people.
They make notes.

They study people's heads...And make reports.

Sometimes the language of the reports is just for other psychiatrists.

Psychiatrists say things like:
Basic behavior patterns are not necessarily caused solely by mass media in whole or part--

If you said that, you would be proud. You would be invited to speak at PTA meetings where you could drink lots of cold coffee and eat little wet cakes.

You'd be just like a psychiatrist...
He has patience.

Not all things on t.v. are bad. Fathers know this.
They watch ball games. *(It must be admitted some of them are bad.)*

Mothers know that not all things on t.v. are bad.
They watch operas and folk singers.
(It must be admitted some of them are bad, too.)

But ball games and operas do not injure
the tender brains of parents. (Nobody
knows the effect of folk singers.)

Parents can find out what is best
for a child to watch on t.v.
If a child is not to be injured, he needs help.

Psychiatrists know
a lot about children.

Children know a lot
about children.

But psychiatrists are not children.

It is hard to dandle one on your knee.
A parent might have trouble.

It is better to dandle a child.
Of course, this could be trouble, too.

But the child might speak your language.
You might even learn to speak the child's.
Then you have established "communication".

You could be most successful saying, in
your own way, that your child has many
influences and chances are he'll be happy
and reasonably normal if you make sure
they are good ones.

You might find out that patient
supervision of shared t.v. viewing would
help your child be *more like himself.*

T.v. watching could be a normal part of a balanced whole. Just like radio, comic books, formal education and love... ... Also milk.

Psychiatrists would cheer you. They believe, most of all, in "do it yourself" happiness....

The Pogo Primer for Parents (TV Division) will reassure and reward any parent who reads it. It was created by Walt Kelly for the Department of Health, Education and Welfare and applies concepts of child rearing embodied in the findings of the 1960 White House Conference on Children and Youth. The primer is designed for parents but children love the pictures. Everyone immediately recognizes the "one-eyed monster," television. Kelly believed that parental selectivity of television fare for children could broaden their understanding of the world. Television is here to stay. This may be considered Kelly's view on how, when and how often he thought children should watch it. A heady question that has continuously baffled many parents.

Another Day . . .

A DAY IN THE LIFE OF WALT KELLY

About 1952 a set of promotional photos was distributed by the syndicate to show tongue-in-cheek how Kelly created Pogo.

Humoring Syndicate Chief Bob Hall . . .

Reading Hate Mail . . .

Ordering in Chinese Food . . .

Thinking About the Okefenokee . . .

Drawing, Lettering, Inking . . .

Sunset . . .

POGO'S HOMAGE TO KRAZY KAT

POGO

".....'AND **WHAT** IS SO RARE AS A DAY IN **JUNE**? THEN, IF EVER, COME **PERFECT DAYS**....'"

THAT'S BY OL' **JAMES RUSSELL LOWELL**.

PEACE AN' **HARMONY** ABOUNDS AN' A FULL STOMACH SITS ON **EITHER** HAND.

HEY!

BIG MOUTH....

HAIL TO THE FIRST DAY OF JUNE, GENTLE-MINTS.

WOW! ME AN' MY OL' FRIEND **ALBERT** IS FOUND OUT WE SHARED A COMMON **ACADEMIWOCKLE** INTER'ST WHEN WE WAS MERE **STRIPLINGS**.

6-1 PUBLISHERS-HALL SYNDICATE INC.

I USED TO READ THE FUNNY PAPER WHAT HAD THE **MOUSE** HITTIN' THE **CAT** WITH A BRICK!

HAW

AN' I USED TO **LOVE** THE "**PUSSY CAT PRINCESS**."

ALL US **LIBERAL DOGS** LOVED TO SEE THAT DOWNTROD LI'L' **MOUSE** CREAM THAT **BIG, FAT CAT** WITH THE BRICK.

YEH, THEM MICE TOOK IT FROM CATS **LONG ENOUGH**.... ALL US **BIG LIBERALS** WAS FOR THE **UNDERDOG**.....

BUT S'POSE THE **CATS** WERE TO TURN ON THE **DOGS**?

IN THE **FIRST** PLACE A **CAT** IS NOT OF SUFFICIENT **MENTAL CALIBRE** TO....

AAARGH! **HAND** ME A BRICK.

EVERYBODY'S FOR THE UNDERDOG ...LONG AS HE **STAYS** THE UNDERDOG.

THE S.S. DICK CHAMBERLAIN

CALIFORN

© 1969 WALT KELLY

POGO

BEAUREGARD, YOU GOTTA DO SOMETHIN' ABOUT THAT BRICK THROWIN' RASCAL CAT.

THE **BEST BRAINS** IN THE COUNTRY URGES YOU TO **FLEE THE COUNTRY.**

WHAT BEST BRAINS?

OURS!

YEAH, HIS AND MINE BRAINS! **NEW!** HAR'LY BEEN **USED!**

WE BEEN THINKIN' 'BOUT YOUR PROBLEM WITH THE BRICK THROWIN' CAT.... YOU GOTTA **LEAVE THE COUNTRY**.... WE'LL SACRIFICE ALL AND **OUTFIT** YOU FOR THE **JOURNEY,** BEAUREGARD.

I'LL DIG OUT SOME **PROVENDER** THIS INSTANT.

7-13   PUBLISHERS-HALL SYNDICATE INC.

AN' THEN...

I'LL LEAVE THAT PIE TO COOL AND FETCH SOME OTHER ...

THUS, FULLY PROVIDED, YOU CAN WANDER THE PATHS OF THE WORLD....A **MIGRANT WILLIE THE WISP**...HAPPY, ALIVE....

A SONG ON YOUR LIPS... ...THO' **HOMELESS**... (SOB) HIC.... HINK!

THE PIE'S **GONE!** SOME **THIEF** IS EAT IT!

YOU GOT *HICCUPS!* YOU ET THE PIE.

THEM'S MY **OWN** HICCUPS....BRUNG 'EM FROM HOME.

ARAGH! YOU BOLGOTCHIN' LOGGARAZZLE ROGHK!

AARGH

HIC!

© 1969 WALT KELLY

— 104 —

WALT KELLY KNEW THE IMPORTANCE OF SPECIAL POGO DRAWINGS TO BOTH HELP A WORTHY CAUSE AND KEEP POGO IN THE PUBLIC EYE.

'Trick or Treat' Collection For UNICEF Here, Oct. 31

TRY YOUR TRICKS AND TREATS FOR UNICEF THIS HALLOWE'EN

OPEN YOUR DOORS AND HEARTS...

TO ALL THE WORLD'S CHILDREN
Please — Pogo

CONGRATULATIONS, GASTONIA!
"ALL-AMERICAN CITY"

FROM POGO AND ALL THE SWAMP CRITTURS INCLUDING WALT KELLY

I CAN HELP.
HERE IS A CHECK FOR THE SALVATION ARMY at 121 W. 14th ST., N.Y. 11, N.Y.
I CONTRIBUTE $_____ TO THE **1953** FUND

(CHECKS PAYABLE TO THE ARMY. RECEIPT WILL BE MAILED FOR YOUR CONTRIBUTION WHICH IS DEDUCTIBLE FROM YOUR INCOME TAX.)

SUMMER PROMOTIONAL ART, 1962 and 1966

From The Hall Syndicate, Inc.
    30 East 42nd Street, New York 17, New York

Suggested copy for POGO vacation ads.   One-column mats for the art in
these ads are available to POGO subscribers on request.

Phone (NUMBER) and
arrange to have
(NAME OF PAPER)
mailed to you daily
--complete with POGO
--at your vacation
address.

(NAME OF PAPER)

Phone (NUMBER) now
and arrange to have
us mailed to you at
your holiday address.

(NAME OF PAPER)

Phone (NUMBER) now
and arrange for your
vacation newspaper
to come to you daily at
your holiday address.

(NAME OF PAPER)
-- with POGO --

A phone call to
(NUMBER) will
arrange delivery

(NAME OF PAPER)

and your favorite
comic along on your
vacation. Phone
NUMBER now and arrange
delivery.

"POGO"
    'n'

(NAME OF PAPER)

A phone call to
(NUMBER) will
arrange it.

From The Hall Syndicate, Inc.
   30 East 42nd Street, New York, N.Y. 10017

Suggested copy for POGO'S hilarious trip to "Mars". Your readers will not want to miss this amusing summer sequence. These ads will encourage them to have your newspaper follow them on vacation.

Use week of July 4	Use week of July 11	Use week of July 11

MOST OF THE FUN IS BEING THERE

WITH *POGO*

So phone (NUMBER) and arrange for POGO in (NAME OF PAPER) to be with you all summer -- wherever you are!

WHO COULD FORGET AN *ELEPHANT*?

TAKE ME AND *POGO*

Phone (NAME OF PAPER) (NUMBER) and arrange delivery to your vacation address.

TAKE US ALONG

WITH *POGO*

in (NAME OF PAPER). A phone call to (NUMBER) can arrange delivery to your vacation home.

Use week of July 18	Use week of July 25	Use summer anytime

LIKE TO MEET ME ON VACATION?

I'LL BE WITH *POGO* AND

all of you who call (NUMBER) to invite POGO in (NAME OF PAPER) to your summer hangout.

YOU WOULDN'T *DARE* TO LEAVE *ME* BEHIND...

I'LL SEE YOU WITH *POGO*

Call (NUMBER) now, and arrange for me and (NAME OF PAPER) to be delivered to your vacation address.

LONG, HOT *SUMMER*?

NOT WITH *POGO*

Call (NAME OF PAPER) (NUMBER) and arrange to have POGO to relax with all summer, wherever you are.

WEATHER EARS:

PROMOTIONAL POGO ART FOR PAGE ONE WEATHER NEWS

BREEZY

CHILLY

COOLER

SLEET AND HAIL

LIGHT SNOW

WET OR ICY

SNOW

THESE CAPTIONS ARE ONLY SUGGESTIONS — YOU CAN GET A VARIETY OF USES IF YOU CHOP OFF THESE AND SET YOUR OWN —

COLD

COLDER

SNOW

BREEZY.

COLD

COLD AND WINDY

SLIPPERY

SNOW

SLIPPERY

COLD & FAIR--

FAIR

PLEASANT

FAIR

COOL AND FAIR

WARMER

HOT

HUMID

HUMID

POSSIBLE
RAINBOWS

CLEARING

FINE-FAIR
BRISK

CLEAR

MILD-

SUNNY

WARM

HOT

HOT

STEAMY

THREATENING

CLOUDY – FOGGY

POSSIBOY – WET –

DRIZZLE

SCATTERED SHOWERS

SMALL SHOWERS

SPRING SHOWERS

WET

FOGGY ..... UNCERTAIN

MISERABOBBLE

DAMP

THUNDERSTORMS

RAINY

WET - POSSIBLE STORMS

THUNDERSTORMS

BLUSTERY

SUDDEN WINDS

MAN! I'M GLAD WE GOT BOUNCED OFF... THAT HORSE IS GONNA CHASE THE COW FOREVER YET.

NO... THE HORSE QUITS AT FEEDIN' TIME... GOES RIGHT TO THE BARN.

HOW ABOUT THE COW?

SHE PUNCHES OUT AT NOON SHARP.... SHE'S A SEMI-PRO SOFT BALL PLAYER IN THE AFTERNOON.

I DON'T SEE WHY *YOU*, AS A DOCTOR, CARRIES YOUR MEDIWOCKLE KIT ALL THE TIME.

IN CASE OF AN EMERGENCY.

SUCH AS?

S'POSE A *FAMINE* SUDDENLY STRIKES THE LAND?

6-13   PUBLISHERS-HALL SYNDICATE

I'M STARVIN'!

IN A *TRICE* THE DOC OPENS UP HIS TRUSTY EMERGENCY KIT...

AN' *BEHOLE! LUNCH!*

LUNCH?

YOU CALL OL' DRY CHICKEN BONES AND A SALT SHAKER LUNCH?

THERE'S ONLY *TWO* OF US... *HEY!* YOU'RE SPILLIN' THE SALT! *THROW SOME OVER YOUR LEFT SHOULDER!*

YOU AND YOUR SUPERSTITIONS!

HOW 'BOUT *YOU?* TODAY'S THE 13th.

FRIDAY 13 COME ON A SUNDAY THIS MONTH?!

THAT'S THE *WORST* DAY IT COULD COME ON--- SQUASH DOWN ON THE LID HERE AN' SNAP ME IN UNTIL *TOMORROW.*

YOU'RE MESSIN' UP THE SPARE CHICKEN BONES!

© 1971 WALT KELLY

Christmas 'Countdown' With Pogo & Friends

A POGO CHRISTMAS

Surprise! We have found a new half verse of "Deck Us All With Boston Charlie." The other verses are all reprinted in *The Best of Pogo* (1982). Pogo and Christmas are both special. What could be better than to reprint a selection of dailies and Sundays from the Christmas season.

Release for week of December 21, 1953

— 133 —

Release for the Week of Dec. 20, 1954

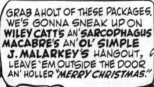

Release for the Week of December 22, 1958

God rest you merrie, Gentlemen~

THE POLITICAL DOPE
AS TOLD TO WALT KELLY
BY POGO
COPR. 1952 WALT KELLY

GUESS **WHO** IS BEING SENT TO **CHICAGO** AS **OUR SPECIAL CORRESPONDENT**

The political conventions of 1952 gave Walt Kelly a natural vehicle for promoting Pogo. The artwork reprinted here accompanied Kelly's observations of the conventions in 1952.

**RARE
PHOTOS
OF POGO'S
(UN)OFFICIAL
CAMPAIGN
HEADQUARTERS,
CHICAGO, IL.,
JULY 1952
AT
COLLEGE OF
COMPLEXES
1651 NORTH
WELLS ST.**

College students, circa 1952, knew the best place to have a convention campaign headquarters was a bar.

Kelly autographs promotional drawings of Pogo.

POGOGATE: "NEWS" ITEMS PLANTED IN THE PRESS ARE REVEALED

CANDIDATE SEEKS GROUND-HOG VOTE

Pogo Possum Courts Critters

Prairie Dog, Wyo., Augtember 97 (Special Dispatch) — Labor leaders here expressed themselves today as being in favor of the plank to make "Ground-Hog Day" a national holiday, a move endorsed by Pogo supporters. "If the possum becalms the President of the United States, it will be our bounden duty to see to it that animals everywhere come into their own," said one operator of seventy five prairie-dog hills employing an estimated 346 workers.

Asked if he had not meant "becomes" instead of "becalms," the Prairie Dog Operator said, "No comment."

An undercurrent of revolt, however, was seen by some observers in the fact that the working prairie dog had not been consulted on the matter. "We work all year long," said one who was incapable of identifying himself, "and the Ground-Hogs sleep. They get up and do one day's work, which most of the time scares them half to death, and they get a day named after them. In fact they are now being told that they can have THAT day off. When we ask for a day off all we get is the Mary Haha. We are told we can go whistle."

On the other hand, Pogo Poll Takers have reported that Ground-Hog enthusiasts have set

OWL CITY HOOTS FOR POGO

Owl City, New Braska. June 59, 1935 (Special) — The cry of "Hoot Mon!" rang across this prairie town today as a convention of Owls, many with decided traces of Scotch in their brogans, endorsed the Okefenokee Possum, Pogo, for Superintendent of Garbage in Beanfry, North Kadota. A brooking group of Liberals, Owls who refused to give a hoot, lodged a strong protest movement on the grounds that the job had originally been offered to a pig. "You do not have to be a pig to be a pig!" pointed out Ahem Koffigan, prominent garbage lobbyist. "We offered this job to the best man available. We believe that so far as general "pig" ability is concerned, Pogo is about as piggy as they come."

What effect this new demand on the popular Possum's time will have is at this p;oint debatable. It was rumored that Pogo, if elected President of the U.S. would appoint a Federal Garbage Counter as one means of retaining his constituency in Owl City and in Beanfry. "We are proud of the activity shown in Owl City and in Beanfry," declared Pogo in an off-the-cuff address before garbage workers. "We have seen other places wrestle with the ever-present problem of garbage and we have seen a great many vast communities come a cropper on the issue. But when we look at Owl Cit, we see a *real* dump. Owl City can be proud. And Beanfry

has a collection second to none. Each city has an atmosphere of its own."

Authorities and others familiar with parliamentary law are both plussed and nonplussed on the subject. Some have pointed out that if Pogo were elected President there would be nothing to prevent him from resigning his duties as Chief of State to take over the job in Beanfry. Garbage Producers throughout the world have their noses to the wind, savoring the political breezes. As one, who would not give his name, remarked: "It's Chicago all over again!"

OWLS CONVENE

to music the old refrain, "How much wood would a would wood would if a wood chuck chuck wood would." Ground-Hogs, the wakeful ones, have indicated that the labor problem, which the new move for a National Holiday brings up, is a formidable one.

"We don't get paid for holidays," explained one. "We sleep through Christmas and January First, both usually considered holidays. We don't get them off. We work right on through. Then at the end of our hitch, we get up to round up the winter's work. If it's a nice bright day and we see a shadow, boom, we get another six weeks work. If it's raining, we get laid off with two

weeks notice. Do you call that fair? And now they want to take our last day's pay away, besides rigging it so that the layoff comes about automatically. Who are these lemmings that go around proposing things? Why don't they swim back where they came from? They got labor problems of their own. If we need a holiday, we'll take Christmas at double time."

Essentially this protest has been drafted and is being sent to Pogo headquarters. The Presidential hopeful said that the whole thing certainly made a man think. Pressed on what he was thinking about, the Possum candidate referred the matter to an aide.

EXPERT ANALYZES H.M. Gov't. COMMENT OF "NO COMMENT."

POSSUM CONFUSES BRITISH

London, England, May 453. (Special) Three different houses of Parliament were thrown into temporary stunned confusion today upon the issue of Pogo Possum's candidacy for the Presidency of the United State of America. Trouble started when foreign experts (thought to be Patagonians) stated flatly that Pogo could sweep Hyde Park in 1956. "Pogo," shouted an M.P. from Lower Backstairs, "could not sweep Hyde Park in 1956, 1957 AND 1958. It's a BIG place."

"The issue," it was pointed out, "is not so much a matter of wheter the American Possum will eventually occupy the White House, the question is WHERE DOES HE STAND?" The speaker repeated that he could not make this last p;oint too strong. A member of the opposition party promptly retorted that the p;oint was already too strong. Crumpets straightway filled the air and an elderly Conservative was taken to the hospital with an attack of hiccups.

The Crown, asked for comment by phone, could not be located. Observers felt that there was some significance in this although a minority thought that it meant nothing. "The Crown has not been located since last coronation," declared a bystander, later identified as T.R. Bystander, a Bull Mooser.

One of the Under-Secretaries, Chiffon Bluestarrs, when asked to explain the seeming confusion in this Mother of Parliaments, smiled but said: "No comment." Experts, at work through the long night, trying to analyze this speech, take some comfort in the wan smile which preceded the remarks of the Under-Secretary. If, it was observed, the word No had not been used before the word COMMENT, the entire sense of the speech might possibly have taken on a different shade of meaning. On the other hand, it is quite possible, in the opinion of those here, that the word NO was not used in the strictly negative sense. Some have pointed out that on occasion the word NO is used as a question. This would be quite possible in the language of international politics and diplomacy. To answer a question with a question was Disraeli's forte. Analysts refused, however, to attempt to go into the matter of what was implied by the word COMMENT. "We've gone as far as we can go," said one, in summing up.

Elephants Restless!!

ELEPHANTS TRUMPET FOR POGO POSSUM

Washington, June 32, 1967 (Special) — The mad stampede of circus elephants here last week was viewed today by Pogo, presidential dark-possum, as only the first sign of a growing unrest among animals in general and elephants in particular. "Elephants," said the Swamp Candidate, "should have rights as equal as anybody. Maybe even equaller."

The Okefenokee Possum was indignant on the subject of working conditions and labor practices generally in the elephant business. "Political symbols deserve a special Fair Practices Act of their own," he said, adding that his administration, if installed in power, would put through a bill immediately for seven dollars and nineteen cents. "It's for laundry," said Pogo. "My private linen can be washed in full view of the public. I have nothing to hide."

If things are bad in the elephant business, there is also some concern about the monkeys. Monkey business has fallen off sharply in what, for many other trades, is actually a boom year. Trial balloons, for example, have been booming throughout many sections of the country.

"We have just recently exploded a trial balloon over the island of New South Georgia in the Caspian," said a spokesman for the Pogo Party. "Results indicate that the entire Expeditionary Force sent down to observe the detonation potential was wiped out. The success of the project is therefore in some doubt. Efforts are being made to send down all opposition candidates for the next explosion.

POGO TOUR DEMANDED

Okefenokee Swamp, Ga., May 39½ (by Special Correspondent) — A whirlwind tour of headwaters through the nation was in the offing today for Pogo following widespread demands that the Okefenokee choice for President hit the road. Pogo immediately went into executive session with the weatherman.

"The possibility of such a tour," a source close to campaign headquarters pointed out, "depends on whether the weatherman can guarantee a whirlwind of sufficient impact." The source promised a hurriedly called press conference the moment a decision was reached. Reporters converging on the scene were told that Pogo did not yet have his own plane; that plans were still up in the air, but that several bald eagles seated near the runway had agreed to help if the weatherman was reluctant to stir up a storm. Later in the day, the services of a hurricane named Xenophobia were offered by a Pogo-for-President club somewhere in the Caribbean. Although her telephone number was available, the Women's Division immediately rejected the offer on the grounds that a sister of the twister had once associated with a questionable typhoon.

It was pointed out that opinion on this latest jam had not yet jelled although the raspberry crop was expected to be the best in years.

POGO PONDERED

Paris, Freptober 31. (Special) — The Chamber of Deputies disbanded in an abandoned quandary this evening after an unusually fraughtful session in which the possibilities of a Possum being the next American President were discussed. Grave complications and implications were seen by Member DuCharmegt in an impassioned speech delivered directly after the meeting ended. Member DuCharmegt spoke from a prone position on the floor from notes gathered at a wedding party held earlier in the day. The DuCharmegt speech or filibuster delayed cleaning women from their appointed rounds until dix heures. Laboring circles were grim.

In part, M. DuCharmegt said: "Is it not proper en les circonsstances to say is it not the fact here that is to say that such a personne, le possum, in truth, is in the premiere place an animal particular, peculiar et (that is to say aussi) formidable? He has the teeth long, the tail prehensible. This Monsieur Pogo Le Possum, is it not that he is also like as to the Dodo? He is not so greatly and largement exactment that is to say EXTINCT. It is to say that here in truth is a development extraordinaire. Here, mesdames et messieurs, is the living fossil. Here is something that has been alive in its present state for over 2,000,000 years. He has not change pas. He has not progress pas. Nesslerode? Pas?"

The cheers of the cleaning women (Les Enfants du Paris) were drowned out by the arrival of Les Gendarmes. Les took M. DuCharmegt home in a large basket.

It is not thought here that Pogo's American chances were enhanced

WORM-WATCHERS ALERTED

Baltimore, O., July 72. (More or Less Special) — A noisy demonstration for Presidential hopeful Pogo Possum all but destroyed the outfield grass of the Baltimore Orioles' baseball park here today, when a disorderly mob composed mainly of members of the Oriole Worm-Watchers Society roared through the playing field burning effigies of opposition candidates and threatening such early worms as were not already underground.

The demonstration was touched off when the Early-Worm Association came up en masse just before dawn for a breakfast meeting designed to kick off the candidacy of Clarence Caterpiggle, a journeyman worm, who recently emerged as the favorite son candidate of several underground groups.

The Oriole Worm-Watchers were alerted shortly after the meeting began and advanced upon the breakfast tables with signs and banners, shouting jeers and catcalls. From this friendly start, the

in this River Paradise but it was pointed out by astute observers that the appellation, LIVING FOSSIL, may help the Possum in any French election held in the near future. "Just the sort of material we are used to!" declared an unidentified official of the Metropolitan.

meeting between the two groups gradually deteriorated into a free-swinging discussion. Real trouble started when the hot cereal bucket was dumped on the head of the leader of the Orioles.

Asked for comment later in the day, Pogo said that he regretted the whole thing. "Worms have rights, too," he declared. "They may live underground but that is no reason to keep them from coming out in the open."

Several hungry Oriole Worm-Watcher members were heard to agree but there has been no official comment from the Oriole headquarters.

MELBOURNE MARSUPIALS MEET

FLEMINGTON RACECOURSE, Melbourne, Australia (Bulletin)—Pogo Possum revealed his secret surprise weapon today when, in a speech before a jammed back-room audience of marsupial mice, he declared that he had in his camp, "one Cunning Clovis, a lady kangaroo, known far and wide for her ability to make tea in her pouch and read the leaves therein, thereby forecasting the future." A survey of one, namely of Cunning Clovis, at an early hour this morning revealed that the coming election results in the United States of America will be a surprise. "At least," said Cunning Clovis, "I certainly am surprised . . . it looks from here like it will be Garfield once again."

A spokesman close to P.T. Bridgeport, Pogo's campaign manager, said today that the survey results pouring in from their colleagues indicate that the issue is still a little cloudy. "Too much milk and sugar in the orange pekoe," said Flanders Flagle, a flea who is close to the source close to P.T. Bridgeport. "Cunning Clovis gave it a good try at ten a.m., but was forced to admit that it was a little early." Cunning, reached in a canoe on the water hazard at Flemington, said that ten a.m. was entirely too early for tea anyway.

An experiment will be made tomorrow by a Chinese Professor who will drop rice cakes with the little paper fortunes into the tea. Tried yesterday for the first time with a limited amount of rice cakes, the experiment bore no positive results. "It was pretty soggy prognostication, but it was the first time," said Cunning Clovis. "I, for one, see no trend about to be established merely because the first two fortune papers to be read are (A) 'You will marry a freckle faced boy,' and (B) 'the night wind blows a dark tune. Keep indoors in December.' We need more information than this," continued Cunning, "but, as I say, it looks like McKinley." Asked whether she did not mean Garfield, Clovis refused to elaborate. "It's too early," she said. "It's hardly lunch time."

POGO A HIT IN THE LAND DOWN UNDER

Rushcutters Bay, Australia (Delayed) — This one-time scene of pugilistic glory was enlivened today by a demonstration of extrasensory perception that may advance the cause of the Kangaroo by a good many generations. Faced with the problem of picking the winner of the American Elections contest, Cunning Clovis, female Kangaroo prognosticator, demonstrated in the presence of Pogo Possum, Swamp candidate for the presidency, that the next president of the United States will have either nine or ten letters in his surname, that many of these letters will be "E's", that "N" will play an important part in the name construction and that "S" will have a good deal of bearing on the pronunciation.

These facts came to light as Cunning Clovis brewed two quarts of tea in her pouch into which was then dumped a half pound of Chinese Rice Fortune Cakes. These were allowed to steep for upwards of fifteen minutes. At the end of that period Cunning Clovis, blindfolded, ears stopped with cotton wool, locked in a huge wooden box from which there was absolutely no escape, pulled from her pouch one of the fortune papers and handed the message to an attendant to the tune of muffled drum rolls by the Perth Pounders Artillery Bugle and Fire Society. There was some confusion when Plummet Proudy, the attendant,

AUSTRALIAN LISTENING POST ORGANIZED

looked at the message. His remark that it was very good indeed, in response to a question, clearly showed that the experiment would have to be repeated. This was done and once again the Perth Pounders sounded a majestic flourish as the message appeared in the dripping hand of Cunning.

This time the Chief Judge, a platypus solicitor, opened the paper and read the history-making information. "It is apparent," said the Chief Judge, "that if I read out EXACTLY what the message bears I may not only influence the election in the U.S. and thus destroy the chances of all, includ-ing our marsupial friend, Mr. Pogo, but I may indeed cause the bottom to drop out of the short odds market in which I myself am a heavy holder. Therefore I will just hint at the message here."

At this a noisy group of Dingoes, obviously on hand to merely cause trouble, set up a yipping and wild-west at the rear of the hall and eventually had to be forced out of their seats with a firehose. Once order was restored, it was discovered that the message had disappeared. Cunning Clovis was in no mood to repeat the experiment and so over a few cups of gloomy tea the meeting had to be adjourned.

A number of marsupial supporters were for having a test case made of the incident, charging that the Chief Judge, a montreme when all is said and done, was trying to hide the true information which undoubtedly indicated the winner would be Pogo Possum, a marsupial.

"This is not true," angrily declared the Platypus. "The paper was here in my hand at the moment that the Dingoes set up their howl and now it is gone . . . It is as simple as that."

Pressed by members of the New Zealand press for some indication of the contents of the note, the Chief Judge said, "All I can recall is that "N", "E" and "S", together with a number of other interesting letters, were quite apparent though a little washed out. There was sugar and a bit of cigaret stub on part . . . also some tooth marks . . but generally the message was clear."

Observers here feel that this latest information, extrasensory and incomplete as it is, certainly establishes a trend. The Kangaroo groups are happily organizing a gala party as a celebration of their sudden emergence as an influential political factor. "Kangaroos the wide world over now feel that their rights, so long overlooked, are at last coming into their own," said one prominent marsupial spokesman. Monotremes are quiet on the subject, although one source close to the Chief Judge, when asked if the Kangaroo conclusion was valid, gave a tight little smile and said, "No, (haha) comment." Experts attach some significance to this last remark.

ELEPHANT BUILDERS AROUSED

Bed-of-Pain, Okla., Jan. 76 (Special) — Pogo, Okefenokee's First Citizen and its favorite-son candidate for the Presidency, climbed out of a sick bed today to attack what he called "the twisted truth behind the Elephant Rebellion in the Nation's Capital." In an impassioned speech at the City Zoo, Pogo declared that Elephants, no matter of what party, have a right to decent working conditions and job security. He pointed in indignation to the treatment "suffered by the loyal pachyderms of the opposition." Claiming that old-line symbols were being replaced by the machine-made elephant, hammered together out of rubber, cotton, and "Rube Goldberg clockworks," Pogo called for an immediate investigation starting at the "top" and finishing at the "bottom." Trunk experts from Oshkosh have stepped forward with an offer to "nose out" the matter.

A question from a baboon in the audience, a retired municipal judge, led the candidate to remark with a twinkle in his eye that, "You can pierce an elephant's hide but you can't hide the whole elephant." This was denied by wire immediately by the Elephant Growers Association, manufacturers of mechanical street parade elephants. This group has been under special attack by the fighting possum who has indicated that machine replacements are starving out the regulars (or live-type pachyderms).

"No wonder the younger elephants led the rebellious stampede of 42 circus performers, as reported by the Associated Press. Here they've put these ersatz beasts on wheels and the old-line bull is not only walking, he's working for peanuts."

Peanut growers throughout the south were scheduled to meet tonight in an effort to bring pressure on what was termed "this latest assault upon the agricultural economy of the nation."

WHO IN THE LOVIN' WORLD IS *THAT*, ALL DRESS UP?

THAT'S OL' BARNSTABLE BEAR ALL DRESS UP FOR A *COSTUME* BALL....

OR ELSE HE GOIN' TO A LATE HALLOWE'EN PARTY.

NOPE.... I B'LEEVE THAT'S HIS *WEDDIN'* SUIT...WOULD HE MARRY MIZ BEAR *TWICE*?

PUT IT *THERE*! I'M *ON MY WAY*! SEMINOLE SAM AN' A *FRIEND* IS GIVEN ME A POSITION IN A *VAST NORTHERN INDUSTRY*.

THEM'S THE GUYS WANTED ME TO GO INTO THE *ALLIGATOR BAG GAME* WITH 'EM!

OH, *NO*, THEY WON'T SUBTERFUGE *ME*... CLEAN JOB IN THE *BEARSKIN RUG GAME* THEY OFFERED *ME*... BUT...*YOU*!

YOU KNOW WHAT THEY HAD IN MIND INVITIN' *YOU* INTO THE *ALLIGATOR BAG BUSINESS*!

Y'KNOW WHEN THEY WAS THROUGH WITH *YOU*, THEY WOON'T HAVE BEEN SO MUCH LEFT OF YOU AS *WISSSHT*!

OOH.... I KNOW.

HOO BOY! ALBERT A *MOGUL* IN THE *ALLIGATOR BAG GAME*! *WHOO*!

DID BARNSTABLE BEAR SAY THAT HE'S ABOUT TO GO INTO THE *BEARSKIN RUG BUSINESS*?

?

HMM?

1950 DAILIES

In *The Best of Pogo* the first syndicate promotional piece was reprinted. It featured dailies from Oct. 16, 1950 through Dec. 23, 1950. As numerous dailies were left out of the early reprint books published in the 1950's, we have received considerable mail asking us to continue to reprint daily strips. Thus the balance of the 1950 daily Pogo comics is presented.

2-1

2-2

2-3

2-4

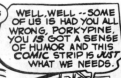

SORRY TO DISTURB YOU DURIN' THE RUSH OF GITTIN' OUT THE SWAMP PAPER, POGO... I GOT A *REE*-QUEST.

WHAT IT BE BUG?

I WANTS TO BE A *COPY*-*READER*--- LOOKY HOW I READS --- HERE'S A 'B' OR MEBBE A 'R', NEXT COME A 'J' AN' THEN A ---WELL HMMM.

LOOK LIKE A PAST PARTISOOFLE WITH A SINGLE WING PLUS A DOUBLE "U" --- WHOLE THING SPELLS "*BAKIN' POWDER.*"

BUG, KIN YOU *HUM?*

AT HUMMIN' I IS EVEN *MORE* WONDERFUL ---HMM-♭-MM HMMITTY-HM ♫ HMMMM HM-MM HMMMM HMMMM HM M

I THOUGHT SO... YOU IS A *HUM BUG.*

YEP, BEAUREGARD, THIS NEWSPAPER DO NEED A *CUB REPORTER*

THEN I'M THE MAN

WHY DOES YOU BRING YOUR OL' CLOTHES HAMPER?

THAT'S WHERE I FOUND HIM.

FOUND WHAT? YOWP!

CUTE, ISN'T HE? SOON AS I SAW HIM I DECIDED TO REPORT

GUESS YOU IS THE WRONG TYPE CUB --- MAYBE THEY WANTS *LION CUB REPORTERS.* OL' SWAMP KINDA LOW ON LIONS RIGHT NOW.

DON'T PASTE ANY OF THESE PICTURES OF WASHINGTON ON OUR PAPER UPSIDE DOWN.

IT HARD FOR ME TO TELL UPSIDE RIGHT ON THESE HUMAN TYPE FOLKS.

I BETTER DELIVER THESE BIRTHDAY NEWSPAPERS AFORE YOU GUMS 'EM UP.

US FOUND A BATCH OF CUTE LI'L PICTURES OF WASH-INGTON THAT SOME-BODY LOST, SO WE STUCK 'EM ON OUR PAPER TODAY.

HOW NICE.

'FRAID WE PUT 'EM ON KINDA SLOPPY --- MAY-BE TH' PAPER'S NOT WORTH THE PRICE, MIS' RACKETY-COON.

JES' YOU NEVER MIND, POGO... I KNOW YOU DOIN' YOUR BEST --- WAIT, I GITS YOUR PENNY.

THERE YOU IS, MIS' POTATO BUG, OUR NEWSPAPER IS ONE YOU CAN READ WITH *FAITH* IN ITS IN-TEG-*GRITTY* AND *HOPE* FOR THE FUTURE.

I SEE SHE SAY IT GONE BE *FAIR* ALL DAY!

BOOM!

Z

'COURSE, YOU GOTTA READ IT WITH A CERTAIN AMOUNT OF *CHARITY*, TOO.

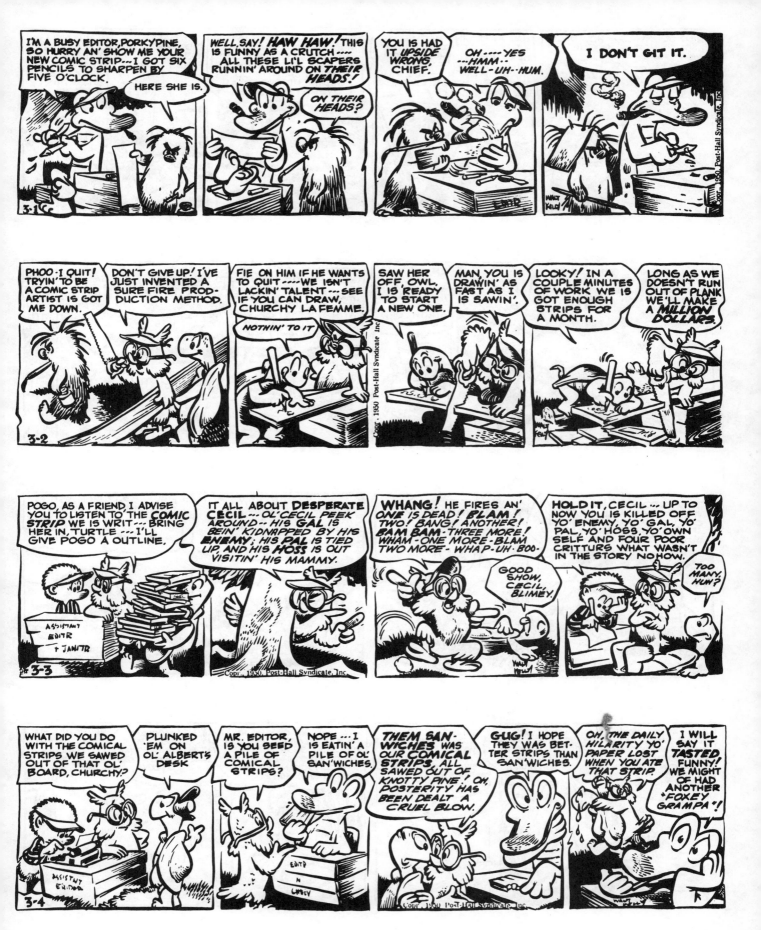

H'LO, DOWNWIND --- HOW'D YOU LIKE TO WORK FOR OUR NEWSPAPER?

NOSSIR!

HAD A COUSIN WHAT WROTE A NEWSPAPER COLUMN AN' HE GOT SO TRIGGER HAPPY THAT HIS OWN FAMILY WASN'T SAFE --- HIS NAME WAS UPWIND OR EASTWIND OR ··W--OOOP!

ANYWAY, THAT BOY WAS MAD AT EVERYBODY --- WHY, HE COULDN'T GET WITHIN ARM'S LENGTH OF HIMSELF WITHOUT HOLDIN' HIS NOSE AN' COVERIN' HIS EYES.

MY SAKES-- DID EVERYBODY OBJECK TO THE POOR CRITTUR?

WELL, NO ---- SOME DIDN'T OBJECK -- BUT THEM AS DIDN'T WASN'T REALLY BREATHIN' NO HOW.

Copr., 1950, Post-Hall Syndicate, Inc.

3-6

GOOD EVENING, GENTLEMEN, I'D JOIN YOU FOR A BRIEF RONDELAY, BUT I'M ON MY WAY TO VISIT AN ACQUAINTANCE, AS IT HAPPENS, A LADY.

WHY. POR-Q-PINE!

THE CATAMOUNT

3-7

OH, SHE'S NO BEAUTY. BUT SHE OWNS THE SQUEAKIEST SEE-SAW SOUTH OF SAINT LOUIS.

I TELL YOU, IT'S FAIR ELEGANT, SOARING HIGH INTO THE NIGHT AIR TO THE MUSIC OF AN UN-OILED SEE-SAW. THERE'S MAGIC IN IT, AND EXERCISE, GOOD FELLOWSHIP AND CULTURE. ALSO, WITH TEN FEET OF YELLOW PINE BETWEEN 'EM, A PAIR OF PORKYPINES CAN BE MIGHTY COMFORTABLE.

OL' PORKY GOT THE SAME TROUBLE IN HIS TRIBE AS I DO IN MINE --- SOME OF MY RELATIVES YOU CAN'T TOUCH WITH A TEN-FOOT POLE-CAT.

Copr., 1950, Post-Hall Syndicate, Inc.

THIS IS POGO'S LI'L PRINTIN' PRESS -- SHUCKS, ANYBODY CAN WRITE FOR A NEWSPAPER IF THEY GOT A LI'L MACHINE WHAT SPELLS EVERYTHING.

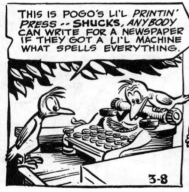

NOTHIN' TO IT --- WATCH!

WOCK POCK

3-8

OOSH! MY SCHNOZ!

SOMEHOW I GOT A SHARP PAIN IN THE HEAD BONE AN' NOW EVERY-THING IS BLACK.

Copr., 1950, Post-Hall Syndicate, Inc.

NEWSPAPER BUSINESS IS DANGEREST --- NO WONDER THEM LI'L SPELLIN' MACHINES GOT SPOOLS OF BLACK BANDAGE ALL HANDY.

EASY, FRED, EASY!

GOOD AFTERNOON, YOUNG MAN, I'M A BOOKWORM BY TRADE, READY TO REVIEW A BOOK, RUN ERRANDS OR ANSWER THE TELEPHONE.

OL' ALBERT AN' POGO HAVE A NEWS-PAPER ---- MIGHT BE THEY NEEDS A BOOK-REVIEWER

TAKE THIS BOOK I RIDE ON, IT'S THE WRONG COLOR ---- AND CHEAP AT THAT. SEE, IT RUNS! DOESN'T RESIST WATER.

3-9

NOW THIS PAGE CHOSEN AT RANDOM, IS LUMPY WITH PUNCTUATION --- HARD ON THE TEETH --CRAWLING WITH CONSONANTS ---- UGH! WHAT SHODDY MATERIAL!

AH, ME! MODERN LITERATURE HAS NO STAYING POWER! SEE, IT WENT DOWN LIKE A STONE.

WHAT WAS THE NAME OF THE BOOK?

OH, WHO KNOWS? I DIDN'T READ THAT FAR.

Copr., 1950, Post-Hall Syndicate, Inc.

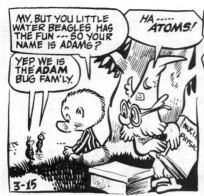

3-15

MY, BUT YOU LITTLE WATER BEAGLES HAS THE FUN --- SO YOUR NAME IS ADAMS?

YEP WE IS THE *ADAM* BUG FAM'LY.

HA..... *ATOMS!*

POGO, IS YOU KNOW THEY IS *MILLIONS* IN MAKIN' *ATOM* BOMBS?

ADAM BOMBS? WHAT DOES *THEY* DO?

WHY, SON, ANY *CIVILIZED* CRITTUR KNOWS WHAT BOMBS DO...

MEBBE I ISN'T AS CIVILIZED AS SOME-- *WHAT DOES* BOMBS DO?

BANG!

THATS WHAT THEY DO.

YOWP!

3-16

THIS NEW CLEAR FIZZICKS BOOK SAY *ATOMS* IS ALL OVER THE PLACE, POGO. ATOMS IS INTO EVERYWHERE.

WHY SAKES! ---- I *NEVER* KNOWED THAT---

OH, OUR OL' ADAM BUG FAM'LY IS *POWERFUL* NUMERICOBBLE.

YEP--- EVERYTHING GOT ATOMS IN HER. SHOES -- HATS-- LIVERWURST--- YEW-RANIUMS-- GEE-RANIUMS---

SO *THAT'S* WHAT BEEN HUSTLIN' 'ROUND UNDER THE KIVVERS COME NIGHT-- BY DIGGY DOGBONE, OL' ADAM BUGS DON'T GOT NO CALL TO BE SO *GREEGARIOUS.*

WHY'D YOU POP THE ADAM BUG FAM'LY INTO THAT BOX?

THEY IS THE ONLY LOOSE *ATOMS* I IS SEED -- I GONE MAKE A BOMB AN' BE A MILL-IONAIRE.

BOMBS IS A PROBLEM, OWL; THEY IS *NO GOOD.*

NO--- THEY PUTS EVERYTHING *TOO* EVERYWHERE AN' IN LI'L BITS, TOO.

3-17

THAT'S THE ADVANTAGE OF THIS TYPE BOMB-- A *ATOM* BOMB CAN PUT *EVERYTHING* ALL OVER NOWHERE! --- NOTHIN' TO SWEEP UP---

NO MUSS, EH?

ABSOLOOSELY NO MUSS--- SOLVES YOUR PROBLEM.

GLAD OF THAT, THO' IT'S NOT *EGGS-ZACKLY* THE PROBLEM I HAD IN MIND.

PSSST-- BUGS, YOU OKAY?

WELL, I GLAD YOU IS FINALLY PUNCHIN' HOLES IN THAT BOX TO GIVE THEM *ADAM* BUGS SOME AIR.

FOOSH --- THIS HOLE IS FOR THE BOMB'S *FUSE.*

3-18

BOOK SAY: WHEN YOU SPLITS AN ATOM, IT--

SPLITS A *ADAM!?* OWL, YOU ISN'T GONE USE THEM FRIENDLY BUGS FOR *BAIT?*

WHAT A IGNORAM-BUMPTIOUS YOUTH! BAIT *IN*-DEED! POGO, YOU JUS' *DON'T* UNDERSTAND 'BOUT *FISSION* A --TALL---

SO!

I KNOWS THIS MUCH 'BOUT *FISHIN'* OWL --- WHEN YOU USES A CRITTUR FOR *BAIT,* IT SORT OF SPOILS HIM FOR ANYTHING ELSE-- AN' I ISN'T GONE *LET* YOU DO IT TO THE OL' *ADAM* FAMILY.

WHY, *POGO!*

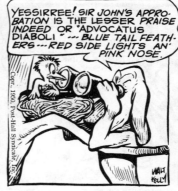

FOR A FEE I COULD TEACH YOUR FRIEND ALBERT HOW TO ACT LIKE A MOUSE ---- THEN THOSE MICE WOULD LET HIM INTO HIS OWN HOUSE.

LIKE THIS...YOU WOULDN'T KNOW ME FROM A REAL MOUSE, WOULD YOU? BE HONEST NOW---- SQUEAK! SQUEAK!

Copr., 1950, Post-Hall Syndicate, Inc.

SQUEAK! SQUEAKIE SQUEAK SQUEAK SKA-WEEK!

SQUEAKITY SQUEAK SQUEAK SQUEAK SQUEAK

YOWP!

YOU, TOO, CAN BE A SUCCESS! TRAIN NOW FOR A CAREER THAT ALWAYS HAS AN OPENING!

WHAT SORT OF AN OPENING?

AN OPENING INTO THE BEST HOMES ----AH, WHAT LITTLE ARTISTS ARE ALWAYS SLEEK, WELL FED, SHELTERED...? STEP A LIT-TLE CLOSER, FRIENDS, I'LL TELL YOU WHAT YOU SHOULD BE...

WHAT? WHAT?

MICE.

WHAT DID YOU HEAR?

MICE.

HUT-TUT-TUT TUT-TUT-TUT-TUT SHOOOOSH! GOOD JUMPING GRANDFATHERS! DON'T LET IT GET AROUND!

Copr., 1950, Post-Hall Syndicate, Inc.

YOU SAY YOU FIGGERED OUT A SONG WHAT WILL DRIVE THEM MICE OUT OF MY HOUSE, SURE FIRE?

AB-SO-LOOSELY.

MY BANG-JO AN' ME IS COMPLETELY UN STRUNG...THE RUNGS IN MY LADDER RING THREE... DO NOT WRANGLE THE WRONGS OF RANGOON, DEAR... FOR THE "GANGRENE" HAS SET OUT TO SEA!

THIS SHOULD DO IT.

MM---BREAD---SUGAR---COFFEE GRINDS---ORANGE PEELS--- --BOLOGNA---BUT NO MUSTARD!

NEED MUSTARD? JUST WAIT!

OH, RING OUT WILD WRANGLING RANGOON MY LADDER RUNGS TIME FOR OUR TEA-LET'S MUNGLE A MANGO AMONG THE MONSOON... WHILE THE "GANGRENE" SETS OUT FOR THE SEA!

OOG! MAYONNAISE!

WALT KELLY

ONLY AN APPROACH BRISTLING WITH PEACE AND QUIET CALM WILL ROUSE THE MICE FROM ALBERT'S HOUSE ---- STRIKE A CHORD TURTLE, I'LL DEMONSTRATE...

HMUM-MM-TUM-TUM "OH, SUMER IS ICUMEN IN, LHUDE SING CUCCU; GROWETH SED AND BLOWETH MED AND SPRINGTH THE WUDE NU. SING CUCCU!"

HELLO?

GOONK

MOUSE CONVENT

SKOOSH!

WELL, CUCKOO, WHAT'S NEW, NU?

AAAAAH--- MICE IS VERY UNPREDICKLISH!

Copr., 1950, Post-Hall Syndicate, Inc.

WALT KELLY

ALBERT, THESE TWO STRANGERS IS UNVESTIGATIN' THE LOST PUP-DOG MYSTERY. THEY ASKS IF YO' HAD ANYTHIN' UNUSUAL HAPPEN LATELY---?

WELL..WHEN I WAS ASLEEP I HAD A REAL-LIKE DREAM! SEEM SOMEBODY FED ME SOMETHIN' AN' I SAYS TO MYSELF, ASLEEP LIKE, "MAN, THAT IS TASTY!"

WHAT !? IN----YOUR-----SLEEP------ YOU---ATE----SOMETHIN'----- AN'----IT-----WAS----WAS---- WAS----- Tasty?

SURE WAS!

THE LI'L' DOG CHILE WHICH WAS SO LOVEABLE ~DEAR AND SWEET~- WHICH DISAPPEARED AND VANISHED --- THAT WAS A LITTLE DOG WHAT GO BY NAME OF TASTY!"

6-9

WELL, HAWGSHAW, THE TRAIL OF THE LOST PUP ENDS AT ALBERT'S HOUSE --- OUR HOUNDS WILL SEE IF IT GO 'LONG ANY FURTHER.

TOO BAD, ALBERT--- YES, THATS TOUGH LUCK.

WE MIGHTY UPSET 'BOUT THAT PUP-DOG, OWL.

OH..DON'T WORRY SO,-- MY DEAR SIR, ----THERE'S VERY LITTLE TO SHOW HE DISAPPEARED INTO YOUR HOUSE!

SO FAR YOU'RE IN THE CLEAR---OH, THERE'S THEM AS WHISPERS THE LI'L' PUP IS BEEN ATE! BUT, NO PROOF YET ---SO, CHIN UP, OLD BOY --CHIN UP!

Copr., 1950, Post-Hall Syndicate, Inc

6-10

FROM WHAT I HEAR, THE LOST PUP DOG VANISHED AT ALBERT'S HOUSE --- 'COURSE ALBERT DIDN'T LIKE THE TAD TOO WELL AN' ALBERT IS A ALLIGATOR BY TRADE.

OH, DON'T GIVE IT A FIRST THOUGHT.

WELL, ALBERT IS MIGHTY WORRIED!

OOG

OH---HE'S MIGHTY WORRIED.. YES-SIR!

THAT'S ONLY NATURAL, HUH, PORKY!? HUH? HUH?

HUH!

IT SHO' IS NATURAL FOR SOME CRITTURS TO ACT NATURAL.

LET'S GO HAVE TEA AN' TALK THIS OVER AT YO' HOUSE WITH CAKES.

YESSIR! MIGHTY WORRIED!

Copr., 1950, Post-Hall Syndicate, Inc.

WALT KELLY

6-12

So! The young dog is lost --- When I was a child it was forbidden to be lost ~~ Oh, this modern youth! Ah, the brave Investigators!

BLOODHOUNDS?

HEY! WHY DON'T YOU TWO USE REAL BLOODHOUNDS?

NOTCHERWELLY, THE BLOODHOUND IS TOO BOSSY---HE GOES WHERE HE WANTS--- FOLLOWS HIS OWN NOSE WITH NO, BUT UTTERWELLY, NO EYE-MAGINATIONS.

WITH WELL-MANNERED DOGS, NOTCHERWELLY, SUCH IS NOT A PROBLEM.

The point is well taken!

THEY CAN'T TAKE IT TOO FAR FOR ME.

Copr., 1950, Post-Hall Syndicate, Inc.

WALT KELLY

6-13

AND, WHILE THE SEARCH GOES ON..

A *PUPPY!* WHAT ARE YOU IN FOR? YOU LOOK KINDA SAD, KIDDO.

WURF!

We find the pup detained in sad and secret Durance Vile.

WANNA GIT *SPRUNG*, SON? I'LL SHOW YOU MY PRIVATE EXIT. IS IT A LITTLE SNUG? ---OOMPH ---I'M AFRAID, MY BOY, THAT, UNLESS WE BLAST, IT WON'T WORK.

6-14

DON'T FRET, OLD SOLDIER, IF YOU'RE *IN...* YOU'RE *IN*-- I'LL GET SOME GRUB AN' WE'LL SPEND THE NIGHT SINGING AND TELLING LIES.

I MIND ONE TIME I STOP OVER IN FRISCO AND THERE'S THE STUPIDEST LOOKIN' CAT SITTIN' IN A BAKE SHOP WINDOW --- *WELL, SIR, I* BLOW ME DOWN! HE'S ASLEEP! WELL, HE'S YOUNG AND NOT MUCH FOR INTELLECTUAL DISCUSSION.

Looking for the lost dog, eh? Well! Every~ one thinks Albert Ate the poor lad~ The Investigators express grave fears ~~~ O! I shall demand custody of the Child! No cannibal is a fit guardian.

6 15

HOW CAN *YOU* BE IN CHARGE OF A PUP WHAT IS *ALREADY ET* BY ALBERT?

~ Well! There's duplicity for you! See how cunning and under~ handed he is? ~

You'll be glad to know there's no need searching for the lost pup any more ~~ The Investigators have decided that Albert ate him ~ Owl will serve as Judge; Turtle and Myself will be on the Jury so we can Convict Albert with a Fair Trial

GOOD! THINGS OUGHT TO BE FAIR.

6-16

IT'S INTERESTING TO KNOW THAT THE *CONFIDENCE* OF *IGNORANCE* HAS NOT DIED OUT!

BIG WORDS OF PRAISE MAKE ME GIGGLE AN' SNEEZE.

You must learn to accept gracefully the plaudits of a grateful community

THERE GO THE INVESTIGATORS TRYIN' TO PIN THE PUP'S DISAPPEAR-ANCE ON ALBERT.

6-17

THEY SAYS THEY IS GOT *PROOF* THE PUP DOG VANISHED INTO HIS HOUSE.

IT *HARD* TO FIGGER

A LI'L' DOG DISAPPEARS NEAR A CRITTUR WHAT COMES FROM A FAMBLY WHAT *EATS ANYTHING.* ---AND *THAT* LI'L' DOG IS *NEVER SEED AGAIN.*

WHAT'S A BODY TO THINK?

I HEARD YO' LAST *REE-MARK*, PORKY---LET'S *FACE FACTS! STOP SHILLY-SHALLYIN'!* THE CRITTUR YOU MENTION *GOTTA* BE GUILTY---HE JUS' *MUST* OF *ET* THE PUP DOG---AN' I DON'T CARE *WHO* HE IS!

HELLO, PARD! I BRUNG SOME PAPER HATS AN' FAVORS----- TIME YOU WAS CHEERED UP WITH A LITTLE PARTY.

6-23

HAVE A COOKIE, KID --- YOU LOOK GREAT IN THAT OUTFIT ----- *CHEER UP!* OPEN YOUR FAVORS.

THIS SHOULD HAND YOU A LAUGH, PAL; ON THE OUTSIDE A COUPLA SNOOPS ARE HORSIN' AROUND LOOKIN' FOR A LOST KID --- *BIG REWARD* AN' ALL --- NEITHER ONE COULD FIND HIS OWN HEAD WITH BOTH HANDS AND A ROAD MAP ----- *HAW HAW!*

WOULDN'T MIND FINDIN' HIM MYSELF ----- YOU AN' ME WOULD BE EATIN' HIGH ON THE HOG, KID.

—Copr., 1950, Post-Hall Syndicate, Inc.

HEY! WHAT'S THE BLEACHERS FOR? A BALL GAME? WHERE'S THEM OL' UNVESTIGATORS?

'TAINT BLEACHERS; IT'S A JURY BOX -- UNVESTIGATORS GONE THROW A BIG OL' TRIAL,

A TRIAL?

OF WHO?

OF YOU.

6-24   Copr., 1950, Post-Hall Syndicate, Inc.

HEY --- FETCH SOME BRANCH WATER!

WHAT'S A MATTER *HIM?*

DON'T TAKE LIFE SO SERIOUS, SON --- IT AIN'T *NO HOW* PERMANENT.

I GONE BE ALBERT'S LAWYER IN THE TRIAL, CHURCHY; AN' DO I UNDERSTAND CORRECT THAT YOU IS IN TRAININ' TO BE A JURYMAN?

YOU UNDERSTANS 100% OKAY.

ALSO I UNDERSTAND YOU IS *CON*VINCED THAT ALBERT IS *GUILTY* ... 'COURSE I COULD CHALLENGE YOU, SIR,

TO A *DOOL?* WODD-EYE-DOO?

6-26

NO, BUT LEMME *TELL* YOU --- IN A CASE LIKE THIS THE *JURY* CAN'T A-GREE ---- AND IF IT CAN'T AGREE, IT'LL BE A *HUNG JURY*

HUNG?

HUNG.

SUDDEN I SEES IT CRYSTAL CLEAR *I* IS MORE THE *IMPORTANT WITNESS* TYPE

Copr., 1950, Post-Hall Syndicate, Inc.

AS ALBERT'S LAWYER, I GOTTA QUESTION ALL THE JURY MEMBERS, MIZ LIMPKIN; I HOPES YOU HASN'T DECIDED THAT ALBERT'S GONE BE FOUND *GUILTY* LIKE MOST FOLKS HAS.

6-27

I MOST CERTAINLY HAS *NOT* DECIDED HE'S GONE BE FOUND *GUILTY.*

GOOD FOR YOU, MIZ LIMPKIN.

'COURSE I MUS' SAY, ON THE OTHER HAND, I CERTAINLY *HAS* MADE UP MY MIND THAT HE COULD *NEVER* BE FOUND *"NOT GUILTY"*

Copr., 1950, Post-Hall Syndicate, Inc.

In the secret dungeon ~

WELL, WELL! HOW'S THE BOY THIS MORNING? I BROUGHT YA' A COMICAL-BOOK TO CHEER YA UP.

7-3

THIS IS GOOD CLEAN FUN -- SEE, THE HATCHET MURDERER DOES ALL HIS WORK IN THE BATHTUB --- WHAT COULD BE CLEANER? NOW HE STUFFS GRANDMA, ALIVE, INTO THE DOC'S STERILIZER! VERY TIDY.

GOOD WORK, KID --- YOU'LL PROB'LY GROW UP TO BE A GREAT EDITOR.

REMINDS ME OF A TIME I JUMPS SHIP IN LIVERPOOL AN' HERE'S A BIG STUPID CAT IN A GREEN GROCER'S SHOP ---- HA, WELL, I ------ SAY, WE MUST BE IN A EARTHQUAKE!

Be of Good Cheer

JUDGE OWL, I GOT A WITNESS WHAT JUS' LEARNED IN SCHOOL 'BOUT LIBERTY, FAIR TRIAL AN' OTHER TRIVIA.

THE LIBERTY BELLE

BUY THEM OL' BONDS

7-4

WELL, UM --- IT'S FROM A OL' DECLARATION --- IT GOES -- UM "WE HOLD THESE TRUTHS -- UM -- TO BE SELF -- MM -- EVIDENT --- UH-- ALL MEN ARE -- UH -- CREATED EQUAL --- UM -- WITH CERTAIN IN -- UM -- INALIENABLE RIGHTS !...

I OBJECT! I OBJECT! THIS IS UNCONSTITUTABLE AN' ...

"THAT AMONG THESE ARE --- UH-- WELL-NOW MM -- UH -- UM --

PSST ... "LIFE LIBERTY AN' THE PURGUIT OF HAPPINESS ..."

SURE 'NUFF, JUDGE, BUT SPEAK RIGHT OUT --- 'TAINT NOTHIN' TO BE 'SHAMED OF.

NOW JUST SUPPOSE WE HAD FOUND A MESSAGE WRITTEN IN SPANISH (BY ALBERT) CONFESSING THAT HE WAS THE CULPRIT!

I OBJECT!

7-5

MY CLIENT CAN'T WRITE IN SPANISH!

ITALIAN?   NO!
FRENCH?   NO!
SAMSKRIP?   NO!

YOU SEE WHY WE DIDN'T FIND A CONFESSION IN THOSE LANGUAGES, JURY? ALBERT CAN'T WRITE IN THOSE LANGUAGES!

A TELLING POINT!

OH, HE'S GUILTY!

WHO?

IN FACT, FRIENDS --- I DON'T 'B'LIEVE OL' ALBERT COULD WRITE A CONFESSION IN PLAIN ENGLISH!

AW, I COULD TOO!

AH! HA!

HERE'S HOUN'DOG'S HOUSE -- MEBBE HE CAN HELP ALBERT.

SPSSST!

WHAT YOU HIDIN' OUT HERE FOR, BEAUREGARD?

SOMEBODY TOOK MY COUSIN'S LI'L' BOY DOG FROM OUT FORT MUDGE. I IS WATCHIN' THAT HOUSE --- NOTICE THEM TRACKS GOIN' OUT? AND NONE GOIN' BACK IN?

7-6

THAT IS PLAIN SUSPICIOUS! SO I WAITIN' FOR THE CRITTUR TO COME BACK.

BUT --- IT'S YOUR OWN HOUSE, HOUN'DOG.

NO WONDER I ISN'T SEED NOBODY COME BACK! I BEEN OVER HERE ALL THE TIME AN' COULDN'T GO BACK MYSELF AND IF I DID GO BACK I WOULDN'T OF SEED NOBODY BECAUSE I WOULDN'T OF BEEN HERE TO SEE ME GO BACK 'CAUSE IT WOULD OF BEEN ME GOIN' BACK AT THE TIME.

GOIN'?

YEP, WAY WAY BACK.

SO YOU'RE BACK? STILL FAT FROM PANCAKES.

YEP---- POGO, I IS GOIN' INTO THE GUARDEEN ANGEL BUSINESS.

'SPOSE, FOR INSTANCE, I IS A FISH HAWK AND IS DIVIN' FOR YOUR FISH---- WITHOUT A ANGEL, YOU IS HELPLESS.

HEY! YOU IS TOO HEAVY!

SEE THERE? THAT'S THE VALUE OF A GUARDEEN ANGEL! IF I'D BEEN A REAL FISH HAWK 'STEAD OF YOUR PERSONAL PROTECTOR, I'D OF SNATCHED THE FISH YOU CAUGHT---- BUT I SAVED YOU BY BEIN' ME!

BUT I ISN'T CAUGHT A FISH YET!

WELL, DON'T COMPLAIN TO ME ABOUT YOUR LUCK---- A GUARDEEN ANGEL KIN DO JUS' SO MUCH.

8-14

BEIN' A GUARDEEN ANGEL AIN'T ALL BEER AN' SKITTLES, POGO---- A FIRST RATE ANGEL IS GOTTA BE JERRY ON THE JOB!

8-15

HE'S EVERPRESENT, VIGILANT AND---- SAY, IT JUST OCCURRED TO ME, A PRIME JOB DONE BY US GUARDEEN ANGELS IS PROTECTIN' KINGS FROM BEIN' POISONED.

SNIFF SNIFF

JES' BLOW ON THAT AN' COOL IT OFF A MITE---- THEN HAND IT OVER---- I'D BETTER SAMPLE IT FIRST, SIRE.

HEY! HOW CAN YOU JEOPARDIZE A POSSIBLE CROWNED HEAD THAT WAY?

BUT WHAT A TRAGEDY IF YOU WAS ROYALLER THAN I IS.

I OUGHTA WARN YOU---- I IS ALWAYS GITTIN' IN DUELS, AN' FOLKS KEEP SHOOTIN' HOLES RIGHT ABOUT WHERE YOU IS, GUARDIAN ANGEL.

WHAT?

8-16

PERHAPS I COULD BE HIS GUARDEEN ANGEL---- HE LOOKS LIKE A QUIET TYPE.

PORKY-PINE? I WOULDN'T ADVISE IT---- BUT DON'T LET ME STAN' IN YO' WAY.

YOWP! A SHARP MAN!

WOW! YOU IS PRACTICAL UNGUARDABLE---- YOU NEEDS PRO-TECTION FROM YOU OWN SELF!

WHO DON'T?

I GOT RID OF THAT PESKY BUTTERFLY WHO WAS PLAYIN' GUARDIAN ANGEL BY TELLIN' HIM THE BUTTERFLIES WAS ALL MIGRATIN' TO NEW SOUTH WALES.

8-17

HE FIGGERED HE BETTER GIT THERE BEFORE THE BIG OL' BULL BUTTERFLIES PUSHED HIS KIND INTO THE OCEAN.

HMMF! GOIN' THE OTHER WAY!---- A PERTY FACE IS TURNED HIS HEAD NORTH.

MEBBE THE BUTTERFLIES IS MIGRATIN' TO MANITOBA.

SHE'S NO BUTTERFLY---- HE DON'T KNOW IT, BUT SHE'S A MOTH! SHE'LL KEEP HIM UP NIGHTS SPENDIN' HIS PAY AN' DANCIN' HIS FEETS OFF.

WELL, HE'S LIGHT HEADED ENOUGH---- MEBBE HE GOT FEETS TO MATCH.

ALL THE PUP-DOG CAN SAY IS "POLTERGEISTS ETC., ETC.,...." HOW YOU GOIN' TO MAKE A BIG SHOW OUT OF THAT?

HA!

I HAVE WRITTEN A PLAY STARRIN' THE PUP----HE PLAYS SIR CECIL----I PLAY KING RUDOLF---CURTAIN GO UP AN' I IS FIGHTIN' A DUEL WITH SIX GIANTS.

WHERE'S CECIL COME IN?

KING RUDOLF WIN AN' GRABS THE BEAUTIFUL MAIDEN IN HIS ARMS THEN HE SING A LONG AND WONDERFUL ARIA----

WHERE'S CECIL?

RIGHT THERE! OL' CECIL COME IN ON THE LAST PAGE----HE GASPS OUT: "OH!" AN' DIES---KING RUDOLF THEN GIVE A BIG FUNERAL ORATION AN' WE HAS A BIG PERIOO WITH KING RUDOLF ACTIN AS HOST AN' KING RUDOLF AN'...

YOU SURE YOU ISN'T OVERLOADIN' OL' CECIL?

9-6

Copr., 1950, Post-Hall Syndicate, Inc.

I'M HELPIN' WRITE A VAUDEVILLE ACT FOR THE PUP-DOG--- KNOW ANY JOKES?

WELL, MY DADDY TOOK ME TO SCHOOL, AND---

9-7

TEACHER SAY, "IS YOU A PARENT?" DADDY SAY, "OF COURSE, I IS APPARENT." HEE-HEE-HEE?

A CORNFIELD JOKE! -- GOOD FOR SCARIN' CROWS.

Copr., 1950, Post-Hall Syndicate, Inc.

WELL, A CROW TRIED TO SELL ME A JOKE HE READ IN ANOTHER COMIC STRIP TODAY.

DISGUSTING! I HOPE YOU GAVE HIM SHORT SHRIFT?

I SURE DID! I TOLE HIM: "COME BACK TOMORROW!" THAT'S WHAT I TOLE HIM!

GOOD FOR YOU! 'COURSE WE COULD OF USED A LITTLE SOMETHING TODAY.

OWL, IF I TELLS YOU A JOKE FOR THE VAUDEVILLE ACT, DO I GIT PAID?

YEP! TWO GUMDROPS PER LINE.

9-8 Copr., 1950, Post-Hall Syndicate, Inc.

THIS IS A FOUR LINE JOKE--- A MAN BOUGHT HIS LI'L BOY A FUR COAT, (THAT'S TWO GUMDROPS)

TWO IT IS.

THE LI'L BOY WORE IT TO SCHOOL, (THAT'S TWO MORE)

TWO MORE.

THE TEACHER SAY: "MY, AREN'T YOU WARM?" (THAT'S ANOTHER TWO) CHOMP

RIGHT--- SIX UP TO NOW.

WELL? WHAT'S THE LAST LINE? THE PAYOFF? THE BOFF?

DING BING IT! I NEVER CAN REMEMBER THE LAST LINES OF JOKES--- CHOMP... CHOMP...

POLTERGEISTS MAKE UP THE PRINCIPAL TYPE OF MATERIAL MANIFESTATION.

MAN! THAT LINE IS DRIVIN' ME CRAZY!

LET'S TEACH HIM HIS ACT.

9-9 Copr., 1950, Post-Hall Syndicate, Inc.

NOW, WHEN WE SPEAK TO YOU AFTER THE MUSIC DIES DOWN, PUP, YOU ANSWER: "I JUST GOT BACK FROM THE ANIMAL SHOW!"

ALL RIGHT--- NOW YOU GOT IT!

HEAR THAT WHISTLE PUFF AND BLOW-- AS WE RIDE ON OUT OF BUFF·A·LO?

HEHLO, JOE, WHAT D'YA KNOW?

POLTERGEISTS MAKE UP THE PRINCIPAL TYPE OF MATERIAL MANIFESTATION.

RACKETY-COON CHILE WANT TO GROW UP AN' BE A *ELEPHANT*-- I TELLS HIM ELEPHANTS GOTTA HAVE A *TRUNK*.

I GOT A TRUNK.

ONLY *THEIR* TRUNKS HANGS OFF THE ENDS OF THEY NOSES--- LIKE THIS.

ALSO ELEPHANTS GOT TWO BIG *TUSKS* WHAT STICK OUTEN THEIR MOUTHS LIKE CIGARS.

EVEN WHEN THEY GONE TO BEDDY BYE?

NOW, HERE IS A PICTURE OF A *MOMMA* ELEPHANT--- WHEN YOU GROWS UP, YOU CAN MARRY A LADY LIKE THAT.

OOP! LIKE *THAT?*

Is FOR ELEPHANT

SAY---HOW 'BOUT ME GROWIN' UP TO BE A *FIREMAN,* UNCLE POGO? WHAT DOES LADY FIREMENS LOOK LIKE?

ABC OWL

Copr., 1950, Post-Hall Syndicate, Inc.

RACKETY COON CHILE TOOK A APTITUDE TEST AN' HE DECIDED HE GONE BE A *ELEPHANT* WHEN HE GROW UP.

WHY NOT A *DOG?*

9-26

THE *DOG,* AS *EVERYONE* WELL KNOWS, IS MAN'S *BEST FRIEND.* HE IS A-LERT AND A-WARE-- BRAVE, LOYAL AND TRUE HEARTED, AND BRAVE, LOYAL AND TRUE HEARTED, AND BRAVE, LOYAL AN'--

HEY!

Copr., 1950, Post-Hall Syndicate, Inc.

YOU *SAID* THAT LINE *TWICE* ALREADY!

ODS BODKINS! MY THOUGHTS MUST HAVE WANDERED.

I HAVE A FEELING WE'RE BEING *FOLLOWED!*

HA! *IMPOSSIBLE!* THE DELICATE EARS OF THE DOG WOULD DETECT IN AN *INSTANT* ANY FOLLOWANCE WHAT *SO* EVER---

HOUN' DOG TOLD THE RACKETY-COON CHILE TO BE A *DOG* WHEN HE GROWS UP ON ACCOUNT OF IT'S SUCH A *BIG HONOR.*

9-27

IT'S A *HONOR* TO BE A *OWL* TOO. OWLS IS *WISE*--- THEY GITS TO STAY UP NIGHTS AN' *HOOT*--- BESIDES, THEY FLIES *GRACEFUL*--- LOOKY AT ME *TAKE OFF!*

YES, INDEED! YOU OUGHT TO BE A OWL WHEN YOU GROWS--- *OOP! SPLOPSH!*

Copr., 1950, Post-Hall Syndicate, Inc.

WHAT *YOU* GONE BE WHEN *YOU* GROWS UP, OWL?

HIS

WALT KELLY

EVERYBODY TELLIN' THE RACKETY-COON CHILE WHAT TO BE WHEN HE GROWS UP, PORKY-PINE ---

GUESS I WOULDN'T MAKE A GOOD *PORKY-PINE,* WOULD I? YOU IS AWFUL STICKERY, AND DON'T LIKE *MOST* FOLKS, DO YOU?

NOPE AN' *NOPE!*

THE PRIDE OF WAYCROSS

9-28

DOES YOU *EVER DAG* YOU *OWN* SELF BY ACCIDENT?

NOPE--- *NEVER* BY ACCIDENT.

WAYCROSS

ONLY ON PURPOSE!

SOME DAYS I DON'T LIKE *NOBODY!*

WALT KELLY

Copr., 1950, Post-Hall Syndicate, Inc.